The Diary of a Human and a Dog (or Three!)

Clare Cogbill

The Diary of a Human and a Dog (Or Three!)

Clare Cogbill has asserted her right under the Copyright, Designs and Patents Act 1988 to be identified as the author of this work.

This book is sold subject to the condition that it shall not, by way of trade or otherwise, be lent, resold, hired out, or otherwise circulated without the author's prior consent.

Locations or the names of individuals have been changed where requested to protect the identity of those people (or canines).

This book is not intended as a source of advice to anyone regarding their animal's health or behaviour. It is the author's personal expression of events as they occurred. The author accepts no responsibility for how others may interpret her work.

Copyright © 2017 Clare Cogbill

Cover Image Copyright © 2017 Connor McMorran

All rights reserved.

ISBN-10: 1540534634
ISBN-13: 978-1540534637

DEDICATION

For Alun Robert (Bob) and Connor Anthony for seeing Lucy and me through this

. . . and Mum

CONTENTS

	Acknowledgments	I
1	Introduction	3
2	The Diary	6
3	About the Author and Other Books by Clare Cogblll	243

ACKNOWLEDGMENTS

There are so many people to thank—but especially those who have stuck around . . . and those who had no choice but to do so. Thank you to those special people (Bob, Elaine, Linda, and Sheena) who have read my words and given me feedback, and Connor for yet another amazing cover.

A huge thank you also goes to those people who have allowed me to include their own dogs as side stories. Thank you all—and I apologize on behalf of Lucy that she doesn't appreciate your dogs as I do.

My dogs have proven their worth time and time again over the last few years, and I guess that was part of the inspiration for this whole book. They helped me to come to terms with the loss of someone with whom I at times had a difficult relationship. I don't consider myself to be any different to anyone else in my grief, just that amid the rollercoaster of feelings there was, and still is, someone equally bereft—a small dog named Lucy.

Introduction

Lucy was never meant to be ours.

We had poor old, people-shy Ralph, the rescued lurcher, and pushy Peggy the rescued ex-racing greyhound, and were quite happy with our two-dog household. While we had deliberately kept that third place in our hearts available *just in case anything ever happened to Mum*, we never truly believed that the *anything* would ever really happen. At least, we didn't think it would happen for a very long time.

This book is not intended as a sequel to *A Dog Like Ralph*, although it does progress the dogs' stories, taking them on their journey towards becoming a group of three being forced to live together in the same home. I imagine that prior knowledge of the dogs' troubled histories would enhance the reading of this book, but it is meant to be a new story—a new look at the relationships between dogs and we humans. It is intended as an exploration of the human-animal bond we share with them as their human companions. In this case, it particularly relates to the consequences of someone dying and leaving behind their beloved dog.

With the three dogs' journey has come much joy, but along with that joy and laughter, some occasional trepidation. As humans we don't often consider our dogs' personalities and how they may or may not get along with one another. We regularly force dogs to live alongside cats, rabbits, and other dogs they may actually dislike. It's probably just pure luck that in the majority of cases companion animals do tend to finish up getting along.

We were entering this new era in our own lives comfortably aware that Ralph loves all other dogs, in that he makes it obvious he prefers dogs to people. Luckily his love for other dogs is all-encompassing, and is extended to include the lovely Lucy and all that loving her entails. Peggy and Lucy, however, love people but only sometimes love other dogs, and until the point when living together was being enforced upon them, they had never really tolerated one another. And that is, perhaps, a gross underestimation!

So, there we were being launched into a situation that was beyond our control. We didn't ever consider any alternative, because with Mum gone, Lucy was coming home with us. We knew the dogs had existing issues with one another that we wouldn't be able to ignore, but we also knew we would have to somehow make it work.

I was determined it was going to work!

Lucy has an element of cuteness with an equally cute face, and yet in that bold, unpredictable terrier way, her mood can change within a moment. She is a dog of contradictions and can be defensive, playful, bossy, friendly, and protective—often expressing these emotions (and more) within a few minutes of one another. At the same time, however, she has that terrier loyalty and curiosity which means she never wants to leave your side. In addition to this, she defends resources such as food, treats, and people to whom she is bonded, with the greatest enthusiasm. I sometimes wonder, however, whether this avid protection of her humans is mainly because they are the givers of the aforementioned treats.

This is mine and Lucy's story, but it is also a tale of how dogs can help you to heal, and how precious this relationship is that we have with our canine friends. It is a story of how grief can get a grip on us, but how in the end having a dog in our lives really can make a difference.

2014

Tuesday May 6th

Everything Changes

Clare

And so, it has happened.

That thing which we had sometimes talked about, even in a morbidly bizarre way, joked about, but that we never thought would happen anytime soon—Mum has died.

I suppose that's the way of things . . . you're born, you live in the best way you can . . . and then you die.

Out of the crumbled embers of our broken hearts has risen Luella—Mum's dear little dog, just Lucy to her friends. Like the rest of us, this small Chihuahua crossed Jack Russell terrier crossed everything else (perhaps a little bit of corgi in there somewhere?), had no idea that on all those occasions when Mum had said, 'Well, you never know the day . . .' that THAT would be the day.

THAT day happened to be three days ago, the 3rd May. It was a UK Bank Holiday Saturday at 9.30am when my brother Martin phoned to say he couldn't get into

Mum's flat in order to take Lucy for her morning walk. A hundred thoughts flashed through our minds, but we thought the most likely explanation was that Mum was in a deep sleep or lying unconscious. We thought that perhaps she had had a fall in the night and simply couldn't get to the door or the telephone.

While Martin waited for the ambulance and police to arrive, he repeatedly knocked on the window and called out to Mum. On the other side of the window, Lucy was barking and whining at him.

As Bob and I drove the thirty-five mile journey as fast as we legally could, my heart grew heavier and heavier the closer we got. When we arrived, it appeared our worst fears of her being unconscious had been much too optimistic. There would be no ambulance needed.

When the empty ambulance left to go and help someone who could be helped, and once we had waved our poor old mum off to the mortuary, Martin, Bob and I sat with the police officer who had been called to help the ambulance service to break into the flat. Martin and I had keys, but keys don't work when the doors are triple security-bolted from the inside. As the police officer ploughed through his sudden-death rhetoric, we listened as much as our shock would allow us.

I suddenly felt very alone. Despite our sometimes turbulent relationship, the person who had been my closest confidante for my whole life had died, and that was going to take some time for me to get used to. We had been in touch with one another practically every single day of my life. And now she was gone.

As I sat there trying to focus on what the police officer was saying, Lucy sat next to me, desperately pushing her body into my side. She trembled and panted, her dark pink tongue emitting the heat from her body. Her lips were peeled back to reveal her equally-dark pink gums, and her sparkling white teeth that had recently been cleaned by the local veterinary surgeon. The front of her right mandible revealed the space where her fractured canine tooth had once been. We've never known how her tooth fractured—she was a rescue dog who arrived like that.

My attention being distracted by her mouth, teeth and gums there, on that day as we sat on the sofa, made me sad, and made me long for the day to be twenty-four hours earlier when my mum, Lucy's person, had still been alive. I wanted to return to a normal day like the day several weeks earlier when we had collected Lucy from the vets, and brought her back to Mum's flat to sleep off the anaesthetic. I wanted to return to a time when I could still say all those things I wanted to say— the things I wish I had said.

On Friday 2nd May Lucy's life was exactly as it had been for the previous three years since Mum had taken her from the rescue shelter. And now? Well, how do you explain death to a dog? She'd been with Mum when she died, though, so perhaps she knew? I imagine, despite coroner's reports and the like, that Lucy is the only one who knows for sure what happened overnight from Friday into the Saturday. Perhaps she understands death more than we do?

Perhaps dogs do?

Looking around at the unfamiliar scene unfolding before her, Lucy must have been wondering what on Earth had just happened to her world. What had happened to the old woman who used to keep a bag of treats hanging on the door handle of the kitchen cupboard? To the woman she used to cuddle next to when the television was on? To the woman who allowed her to sleep next to her on her bed? To the woman who cared about every breath or sound that emanated from this little dog's body? What had happened to the woman who loved her?

There was never any doubt that we should take Lucy home with us. She was a part of the family and, even with her odd little terrier quirks, she was loved by us all. And so, once the necessary police sudden-death documentation was done, we gathered our thoughts and our new dog and drove the sad distance home.

This was going to be a new life for Lucy and a new life for our other two dogs, Ralph and Peggy. For three years there had been a sort of truce which had been established after the initial tensions between them were over. Lucy had lived a comfortable thirty-five miles away. It was comfortable in that it was too far for them to have to spend too much time together! Now, here we were about to upset the status quo by bringing a pampered, yet riotous (mainly due to three years of excessive pampering) terrier to live with the much calmer lurcher and greyhound. Ralph and Peggy would much rather spend their days lazing on sofas than expend too much energy; Lucy is their polar opposite—small, energetic, sometimes aggressive, and extremely demanding.

Until now, life for Ralph and Peggy had become locked in an endless routine of walk-breakfast-sleep-lunch-sleep-walk-dinner-TV-walk-treats-bed. They had no need to pay any heed to anyone else, as they were blissfully enjoying their time being the focus of everyone's attention without any intrusion from anyone. Lucy? Well, Lucy absolutely thrives on being the sole centre of everyone's attention.

As we drove home, immediately those familiar anxious feelings of Christmases and special occasions past came flooding back to me—times when we had experienced some anxiety when Lucy and Peggy had been together. I had concerns not only because of Lucy's tendency to be a little bossy, but also due to Peggy's inclination to want to chase other animals. We were not really sure what she would do if she actually had the opportunity to catch one. As we got closer to the house and I thought of that greyhound chase factor, panic rose in my belly.

We were heading full throttle into 'introducing a new dog to the rest of the animals.' This was something I had discussed many times with successive groups of students, but now it was happening for real, on this day—the day that Mum quite unexpectedly, as she frequently said, 'popped her clogs.'

Thursday May 8th

Chaos Prevails

Clare

No one this close to me has passed away since I was five years old and Dad left this Earth and the ripples of all our emotions in his wake. At five you don't have much to do with funerals, but when you're older and 'next of kin', you find that you're thrown into a stressful turmoil of undertakers, banks, pension companies . . . and so on, and so on. I can't believe there is such an extensive list of things to do—I really would never have thought it to have been possible.

Exhaustion has become my friend, because only then am I able to rest. I have to keep on going until that point of exhaustion, just in case I forget to do or say something. I've seen other people having to cope when loved ones have passed away, but I've never really considered how I'd be if I was ever that person at the centre of the coping.

While chaos is prevailing in our home, surprisingly, so far the dogs are just getting on with being dogs.

Ralph has never fully recovered from his past and all that happened to him before he came into our lives. He was found as a stray in England, and was moved to Scotland when the shelter he was in had no space and they were considering euthanizing him. As happens in so many shelters that run out of space, if you're not homed, there's an increased likelihood that your number will be next. Our local no-kill shelter frequently takes in dogs from other regions, and we were all lucky enough that Ralph happened to be one of them.

We're sure he was treated very badly in his pre-shelter life and he has several scars which suggest so—the most obvious one being across his face. He also has vertical scars down his front legs which look as though they could be old barbed wire injuries, and a scar on the side of his rib cage that looks as though it could have been caused by a cigarette. In the time that we've had him we have tried to give him confidence in himself, tried to erase the effects of what happened to him, and attempted to enable him to gain trust in people. It has been an uphill struggle at times, but as the years have gone by we've more often observed that spark in him of the dog he was meant to be. This is when he will suddenly demonstrate a burst of confidence during which he will go up to someone quite voluntarily and wag his tail at them. Those are the times that warm my heart.

He's a dog full of contradictions, in that he's extremely excitable when he meets up with dogs he knows . . . and he especially likes small dogs. In return, small dogs that don't normally particularly like large dogs seem to like him. He play-bows in front of them and dances around them as though they have been his lifelong friends.

With people, on the other hand, even now Ralph frequently exhibits a head-shy recoil if someone approaches him from in front, and we haven't had enough time to warn them not to touch him. With children he is cautious but generally more confident, which makes me think he has never been hurt by a child. He definitely prefers women to men, and he prefers left-handed people to right-handed people—an observation we made really early on because of our son Anthony being left handed, and the positive way Ralph has always responded to his left-handed approaches. The crux is that we suspect whoever hurt him was an adult male, and someone who was more than likely right-handed.

Despite all this, and here, I suppose, is Ralph's greatest contradiction of all—he has an extremely stubborn side to his nature. When we are out walking he has a definite idea of the direction in which he would like the walk to go. There are walks we tend to do on weekdays that are a little shorter, and then other walks which are much longer that we do at weekends or if we have more time available on the weekday evenings. Naturally, as most dogs would (and I'm afraid I have to exclude Peggy the lazy greyhound from this), Ralph prefers the longer walks.

Both walks start from the same point, i.e. our house, and about a quarter of a mile into the walk, the two walks lead in different directions. It is at that point that Ralph digs his heels in and, unusually for him, makes direct eye contact with me, and 'insists' that we go on the longer walk. Me being me, and despite trying to be enthusiastic about the previously-intended walk, I often give in. I guess that therein lies the problem! We try to vary the walks as much as possible now so it doesn't become an issue, but every now and then, even on other walks not related to our regular walk, he expresses that desire to go the other way. One common theme to the way he wants to go is that it is always in a direction which will lengthen the walk.

He did this earlier on today, and with my resolve being quite weak at the moment and my head being all jumbled, I gave in. There's a tight knot in my gut and I feel as though I'm not really truly aware of what's going on around me. I haven't cried—I don't know when to or how to.

The longer walk enforced by Ralph, though, has been a real tonic, and it certainly seems to have helped the dogs in their bonding. That whole presence of a dog in your life makes you go outside; they force you to get up in the morning and go out and exercise. This is just one of the many great benefits of this bond we have forged with them.

Peggy is quite confident in most situations, and even though her past as a racing greyhound was obviously not a good lifestyle for her, I suspect her strength of character helped to see her through. She has certainly fared better than Ralph, or many of the hundreds of ex-racing greyhounds I have encountered over the years through my work. Don't get me wrong, I don't for one minute think she had it easy, just simply that something in her temperament got her through all that happened to her, and she somehow managed to survive the emotional traumas of her racing life.

While Ralph is enthusiastically prancing around to greet all the small dogs we see on our walks, Peggy stands as far away from them as she possibly can, usually facing the direction of home. Because she is always keen to make the walk as short as possible, she will stand with her nose indicating the absolute shortest route we can take. This means that at the point where the two walks go off at tangents to one another, while Ralph and I have our human versus dog conversation about which way will be best, Peggy has frequently already impatiently started to take Bob on the short route home.

Lucy is happy so long as she is with people. She can take or leave dogs, but as she is now being forced to live with other dogs, we just have to get on with it in the best way we know. She has already shown us she can be quite bossy with Ralph, but that she has a certain respect for Peggy, and we simply have to make sure we integrate the three of them so they are all happy. This is my great desire for their future—that they all end up living comfortably alongside one another.

Saturday May 10th

Lost in Paperwork with a Canine Appendage at my Side

Clare

I am so thankful that Anthony is home from university to help. I think his way with dogs being such that he just lets them get on with their being dogs is probably helping a great deal. Any time Lucy bares her teeth at the much bigger, much stronger, Peggy or Ralph (which she has now done several times), instead of simply ignoring what she's done, I panic and immediately react with 'No, Lucy!' I then reach for her collar to get her away from the other dog, thus going against all my training and unintentionally rewarding her with the attention she so craves. Meanwhile, Anthony distracts her with a calming, 'Come on Lucy, this way,' and finds something else for her to focus on. Other times he just ignores them, not deliberately, more because he is thinking about something else himself, and in doing so he inadvertently lets them sort themselves out.

When I look at how they are with him and with Bob, I realize that my current utterly fraught state, along with an inner fear that they will never get on, is exacerbating the grumbles and the snaps. I realize it is *ME*, the veterinary nurse and lecturer in such things, the one who knows a reasonable amount about dogs, *I* am the one who needs to calm down. 'Just chill, Mum, they'll be fine,' Anthony keeps on repeating over and over.

My head hurts so much and feels as though it might burst. I feel unable to go into work. I can't, not until I've organized the funeral and sorted everything I need to sort. That massive knot in my abdomen hasn't moved since last week.

While I sit here swamped by Mum's paperwork, I vow to myself that I shall create our own home filing system which would allow anyone who needed to, to be able to find anything they wanted at any time. Mum was full of sayings, and her repeated chanting of, 'don't put off until tomorrow, what you can do today,' obviously doesn't apply to me, because I'm sure my affairs are in disarray. But, as I sit surrounded by all that paper, I realize that neither did it apply to her!

Whenever I sit down to deal with something important, Lucy insists on attaching herself to whatever document I am holding onto, or whichever envelope I am attempting to seal. All the time she seems to feel that need for direct human contact. While I am composing letters to send to the multitude of recipients who will dutifully respond from their 'Bereavement Department' with '*I am so very sorry to hear of your loss',* she places her head on my lap or lies at my feet.

I didn't realize until now just how many companies have set money aside towards having a specialist department for dealing with the bereft. I am, I must say, just a little impressed by this. The majority of companies have been extremely helpful. Their bereavement departments have fulfilled their compassionate duties with great gusto, but there have been one or two companies (usually the ones without such bereavement departments) that have greatly infuriated me with their persistent red tape-inspired bureaucracy. I have even considered a 'name and shame' on social media about one bank I've had to deal with. This has been to the extent that earlier today I composed something ready to post online, but then as my finger hovered over the 'post' button, I had second thoughts. What about being sued? I figured in the end it was not worth the effort; that I was possibly still feeling very emotional; and being emotional was perhaps not the best time to put up an angry posting (with detailed attachment), aimed at 'The Man'

Sunday May 11th

Memories of Rusty—and Cats and Cockerels

Clare

I feel I can't think about anything else except what I need to do now. I can't plan for anything beyond funeral day. We still don't know when that is going to be—there's been a delay in moving Mum from England to Scotland. While I spend most of my time with the phone to my ear, or preoccupied amid the pages of a huge pile of letters, if our new little dog is not sitting on top of those letters, she is weaving her way around us, Ralph, and Peggy.

With it being a Sunday, most of the official departments have been closed, so I spent some time sorting through photographs to find a few we can put on the hymn and readings booklet for the funeral. Looking at the photographs makes me realize to what extent Mum's whole life can be segregated into the eras in which she loved each of her dogs. I have found many photographs of her array of different pets, and I'm becoming much more aware of how different Lucy is to the previous dogs Mum loved during her life. And there was indeed a succession of dogs Mum loved before Lucy came along:

As a child I was frequently shown the faded black and white image of Rusty, the Border terrier-like dog. Mum used to explain that the grey shadings of Rusty's image were so because of his wiry, ginger coat.

I hated hearing about Rusty, because poor old Rusty met an extremely sad demise. He was a victim of 1940s post-war ignorance of animals' needs; a time when they were quite far down society's list of priorities. People were pulling together the remnants of their families and trying to make a world in which they could be happy and at peace. Unfortunately, Rusty's repeated barking was in breach of such peace and upset the people who lived in their street. Thus, then just eight years old, Mum was instructed by my grandparents to take Rusty to the local veterinary clinic to be euthanized.

Returning home, broken-hearted and with Rusty's collar and lead in her hand, she never fully recovered from the events of that day. Euthanasia is sometimes too easy, and while these days an eight-year old would not be allowed to do such a thing, it seems as though back then no one blinked an eye at such an awful experience for a child, or at the moral argument against his euthanasia.

The story of Rusty was told to me hundreds of times and I truly believe that what happened that day scarred Mum. It was perhaps a turning point in her life that made her bestow even more love on the dogs she shared her life with as she got older. Unfortunately, the story of Rusty's tragic end is not the only one to have emerged from that era in the family's dark pet-keeping history.

They had many animals during Mum's youth and, not being particularly keen on animals, my grandmother would cringe whenever my grandfather turned up with yet another stray dog or cat. This was the odd thing about my grandfather, because he actually adored animals and had a great gentleness towards them. As I grew up and demonstrated the love that I, too, have for animals, I was often compared to my grandfather, who unfortunately died the year before I was born.

My grandparents had an organ tucked in the corner of the front room of their Victorian mid-terraced house. Their evenings would be spent with my grandfather playing it or his trusted old accordion, and they would all laugh and sing together.

None of the animals he picked up from the streets were neutered and, as animals do, they procreated—particularly the cats. Once ready to give birth, the queen cats would search for somewhere nice and cozy to have their kittens. Invariably, this would be in the back of the organ. Unfortunately for the tiny kittens, though, once they were born my grandfather would take them to the River Rea, the gentle river that flows behind the rows of terraced houses, and drown them. I dread to think of how many kittens found their way into that river from the terraced houses along that road.

My mum and aunt repeated the stories about the cats,

usually piggybacked to the story of poor old Rusty, so many times during my childhood that I felt I knew all of them. There was unfortunately, however, another story repeatedly told that still resonates with me—the story of Gregory—Gregory Peck!

Gregory was the pet cockerel Mum and her two siblings had as a pet when they were children. Gregory lived in the back yard and he, too, met a premature end. Apparently his fate was similar to that of poor old Rusty, only Gregory's crime was cock-a-doodle-doo-ing at the break of dawn. When people living along the street complained that the cockerel was disturbing their sleep, noisy old Gregory found himself in the pot. More than sixty-five years later my aunt still tells of the injustice of Gregory's end, and how she steadfastly refused to eat anything on the weekend that Gregory was consumed by the family.

I recall being told those stories time and time again when I was young, and as I write this I still feel the horror I felt as a child that someone related to me would do such things. Challenging Mum about it, she simply passed these events of her childhood off as being what everyone did back in the old days.

As I said, and I repeat it here to reiterate, my grandfather was a kind man. I have been told so many times that he was the kindest man you could hope to meet, but when I think about Rusty, Gregory, and the kittens, it does make me wonder whether that truly extended to the household pets. But then, as Mum so often said to justify his actions, and I know it doesn't excuse all that happened . . . those were different times.

We talk of those years as being a time for regeneration; of them being a time when people could gradually recover from the war and all its destruction. Many of those people who lost loved ones had lived through two world wars. I imagine the plight of a dog, a few litters of tiny kittens, or a cockerel doing what cockerels do, seemed to many people insignificant when compared to the suffering that had gone on in the preceding years. It's a shame, but again, I suppose that's the way things were back then.

Monday May 12th

More Canine Companions—Paving the Way for Lucy

Clare

Mentally I am in some weird place. I feel I am floundering while some organized semblance of my real life seems to be going on around me. Last night I eventually had to put the photographs to one side. When I'd started looking at them I felt somewhat detached, but the more I looked, the more I found the images were upsetting me. Today, though, I decided I had to fight it all back as I really have to find those pictures of Mum for her funeral order of service sheet. Once I've done that, I can file the rest of them away for a while and look at them again at some point in the future; some time when it doesn't hurt so much.

There are photographs in the box of Mum with Dad when they were both young and care-free. They're in swimwear and playing with a large ball with another couple on a beach somewhere. They look so full of life and full of anticipation. I look at them and I wonder what is going through their minds. What, then, did they expect their lives would be like? For those moments, on that beach, were they truly happy, completely in the moment? At ease with the world? I've tried to make out where the beach is, but it could be anywhere. I know it is silly to want to know exactly where it was and who they were playing ball with, but now I can no longer ask her. That moment is lost in time and has become secreted away with all the other faded histories of generations before.

For Mum, after Rusty there were many more dogs in her life, and I do now wonder how much that was her atoning for her family's ills. There are photographs of most of them in Mum's collection and, for now, I shall mention those who were very much *her* dogs. These were all rescue dogs that she loved and who arrived in her life from the time of her meeting my dad. These are dogs I knew personally; dogs who were special to me, but perhaps from a much more distant perspective than they were to Mum. My own dogs came later on.

These dogs are the ones that eventually led to Mum going to the rescue centre to pick up little Lucy. There were quite a few of them over the years and each of them had their own story:

Susie came along when Mum and Dad were newly-married. Dad had been horrified to discover that this pretty black and tan mongrel with the wavy coat was being kept in a cloakroom cupboard while her previous owners were at work. This was the late 1950s and attitudes towards animals were still pretty poor, but luckily for Susie the other people were only too willing to give her away. So one evening Dad came home from work with this black and tan, medium-sized friendly dog in the back of his work van. Mum hadn't at that point wanted a dog, but one wag of the tail from this happy canine, and Susie was immediately a part of the family. She stuck around until she died at the age of fourteen, having seen my parents have first my brother, and then me.

Our semi-detached home had its sitting room at the rear of the house. It had French windows overlooking a large back garden, and long flowing curtains. That room and those French windows are ingrained in my memory as being pivotal to so many things that happened in that time-frame: the four of us and Susie the dog living contentedly as a family; those long hot summers and just as lengthy freezing cold winters; Dad having to go onto kidney dialysis; Susie passing away; a new dog, Sheba, coming into our lives; Dad dying; and then, perhaps too quickly in hindsight, Mum remarrying. We lived there for only five years, but during those five years so many changes happened—there was so much love and happiness, but then the worst despair and heartache.

Sheba arrived in our lives after Susie had passed away. Dad had hated not having a dog in the house, and so, one day on his way home from work he dropped by the Birmingham Dogs' Home to find another rescue dog. He was already on kidney dialysis and dialyzing for seventeen hours three times a week, and the last thing we probably needed in our lives at that point was a new dog. But he was still working pretty much full time and, I guess, had instilled deep within him an innate survival instinct, one which would not allow him to even consider he might die. I suppose he just felt as though he was normal and, at that time anyway, 'normal' people would be able to go and get a dog from the rescue kennels whenever they wanted. For him to be unable to do so would have meant something was wrong—horribly wrong.

Sheba was a tall, gangly German shepherd cross. She was a nervous dog and looked ferocious, but she had the softest heart. She loved us all, but mostly my dad, and when he succumbed to that awful illness and died within just eighteen months of her coming into our lives, she was devastated. Mum tried to keep her, and she did, until she met my stepfather-to-be. He had three children, one of whom was allergic to fur, and because of this they made the decision that Sheba had to go. And so, poor Sheba was taken to the rescue kennels and never heard of again. As a child I used to get night terrors and wake up crying wanting to know where Sheba was and what had happened to her. At the time, Mum used to pacify me by telling me Sheba had gone off to become a police dog. It wasn't until more than twenty five years later that she finally admitted she didn't know for sure what had become of her. I only hope Sheba found a family that was better able to care for her.

Mum harboured a lot of guilt over Sheba, years of guilt in fact, and always wished she had found a way of keeping her, but you can't go back, you can't re-write your life and change the things you did so long ago. We all have deep regrets, and Sheba's destiny and the part Mum played in it was one of the things she could never go back and change—something she could never put right.

When I look back, I find it strange that Dad would have chosen such a large, potentially ferocious (but absolutely not so) dog as Sheba. The story goes that he had walked into a kennel yard full of unwanted dogs, gone straight up to Sheba and opened her mouth to have a look at her teeth and gums. The kennel staff must have thought he was bonkers, and there are indeed other stories which support that fact, but having looked inside her mouth, he told them she was the one he wanted. So Sheba made the journey back to our home in the back of his Automobile Association Minivan. He really was simply on his way home from work and just stopping off to see whether he could find a dog to fill our house with love in the way Susie had done. There were no home-checks in those days, so such decisions were unfortunately far more spontaneous, with little thought given to the consequences.

Retrospectively, I now think that he was providing us with protection, and while he didn't know for sure he was going to die, his close friend who also had kidney failure had recently died. I imagine that had shaken him and made him think much more negatively about his own situation. I suppose he thought that by giving us this huge dog, we would all be okay, even if he wasn't going to be there to take care of us.

In the late summer of 1970, the year before he died, my aunt was sitting watching Dad as he was tending the roses in the garden at our house with the French windows. He was out there with Sheba, and this loyal dog lay patiently beside him while he plucked dead roses from their stems. Occasionally he stopped to inhale the scent of the flowers that were still blooming. He was singing, and my aunt continued to sit on the arm of the chair just inside the French windows, listening to his tuneless rendition of Louis Armstrong's '*What a Wonderful World*.' How can a song be so beautiful, melancholic, and happy all at the same time? She thought it strange that he must have known that he could die at any point, they *all* knew, but for those moments, in that garden beyond the French windows, he was safe, he was in some kind of paradise. Just months later, his fate, and that of Sheba, were sealed.

Mum remarried two years after Dad died and we didn't have another dog for about five years—remembering of course the apparent fur allergy of my new step-sibling. At the point when Mum and my stepfather decided we could have a new family dog, the mysterious allergy seemed to disappear. Goodness knows why we, in our strange, malfunctioning step family, decided we could have a dog.

Enter Prince—a dog who, after all, was very much loved by all of us. Dogs do that, they unite people. While he was, indeed, a family dog, while we were all at school and my stepfather at work, Prince spent all of his time with Mum. He was a crossed black Labrador and we all adored him. He had come to us as a puppy from the local rescue centre and was an excitable bundle of love. Like Rusty, however, he too met a premature end, but this time through illness.

Prince was epileptic, quite severely epileptic, in that his seizures were lasting longer and longer as he got older. It had got to the point that they were happening every day, often several times a day. One very grey day, the vet recommended he be put down. And so, at the age of only three, when he had enjoyed just three summer holidays with us and only three Christmases, Prince—'The Black Prince' as we called him, was euthanized to stop him from suffering. Mum and my stepfather were told back then that the treatment could be worse than the convulsions.

With Prince gone Mum found the house to be incredibly empty. She was a housewife, staying at home minding the house and preparing food for the masses of kids we had become when she and my stepfather had got married. There were only five children, but it often felt as though we were more. When we were out at school and my stepfather at work or on the allotment, Mum was there missing everyone. Having a dog gave her the company she needed. With her beautiful Black Prince gone, she became desperate for another dog.

This was where Beauty entered all our lives—'Black Beauty.' Although she was mostly black, she had brindle areas around her face and legs. She was smaller than Prince had been, and that took some getting used to, but she quickly wheedled her way into all our hearts. She had a lovely temperament and was a great dog for a growing family.

I was a teenager by this time and had already decided my future would be in working with animals. I began working weekends in an animal sanctuary, and a couple of years later when I had gained a job as a student nurse in a veterinary practice, one of the dogs I was working with, Chip, came home with me to be Beauty's companion. Chip had a deformed foot but never let it stop her from enjoying herself as she ran around the garden and local parks, flinging her strange leg about as she weaved her way between the man-made webs of trees and bushes.

These two dogs were great together, and now I wonder at the way in which, when I left home, they were separated. I took Chip with me and Beauty stayed with Mum, who was by then divorced. For the rest of their lives Beauty and Chip saw one another several times a week, but I don't know now whether the decision for me to take Chip with me had been the right one. Dogs form strong bonds with one another, grieve for one another when one of their group passes away, and I'm sure that now I would not make that same decision. I imagine at the time I thought Chip's bond with me was greater than her bond was with Beauty, which now seems like a selfish thought to have influenced my decision.

Since that point, however, I have always had more than one dog at a time, so Chip had new friends very quickly, and Mum found a new companion for herself and Beauty in the form of Kerry.

Kerry had been admitted as a stray to the animal shelter in which I was working and I persuaded Mum to take her. So Kerry found her new forever home with Mum and Beauty, while Chip had a new friend called Jessie; luckily the four dogs got on well together, and were closely followed by Fluke, a rescued crossed collie I brought home from work.

Mum's Kerry was a funny little dog—a Jack Russell type who was mostly black but with a white blaze across her chest. She had an overshot top jaw which made her look slightly goofy and, like Lucy, she had that terrier instinct which made her a little unreliable with other dogs. Thankfully, however, she and Beauty adored one another, and she tolerated my three.

Unlike some of their predecessors, all five of these dogs lived for a very long time. Beauty and Kerry became Mum's close companions, seeing her through a lot of life's difficulties, several house moves, and quite severe long-term mental and physical illnesses. Mum never recovered from losing my dad. Yes, she remarried, but there was no way anyone on this Earth could have ever competed with what she had shared with him. Their relationship had not been perfect—few relationships are. I suppose what made it so awful was that he died when they were both so young; she'd had all those expectations of their plans for the future and then regrets over what might have been. In the end it was her dogs that became her world; became her key focus, second only to that of her children and grandchild.

When Beauty was fifteen years old she finally went off her hind legs and we had to have her euthanized. I once heard of euthanasia being described as that one final kindness you can give your dog or cat to remove their suffering. Even though in animals we have this option, knowing when the time is right can be difficult, and many people struggle with knowing when, how, and where to deliver this final kindness in order to make it something you remember as being the right decision at the right time. With Beauty I think Mum got it right, and I think because of that she had no regrets.

Kerry, like her past comrade Beauty, passed away at a good old age. The nurturing and love she'd received for the thirteen or so years Mum had her had been equally beneficial to the two of them. That strong human-animal bond is demonstrated time and time again in the way that dogs enter our hearts and, it would seem, in the way they have taken us into theirs.

With dogs naturally having a much shorter lifespan than we humans do, we are likely to love several dogs in our lives. As I talked about in *A Dog Like Ralph*, if you have multiple dogs at the same time, then you repeatedly have that sense of loss as each one reaches the end of their days. Some people love only one dog in their life, perhaps because they have one as a family pet when they are growing up, or sometimes because they have their first dog when they retire.

When someone does eventually find the right time in their life to love a dog, there can be a sense of being overwhelmed at the strength of feeling they have for their vulnerable new companion. So many people decree that they don't know how they managed in their pre-dog life.

When the inevitable happens and the animal reaches the end of their life, one of the decisions to be made is where the euthanasia happens. There are advantages to euthanizing at home or in the veterinary clinic. At the clinic there are plenty of people around to help and there's easy access to all the equipment you need. It also means that the memories back home of someone's canine companion are all the happy ones and not the dog's final moments.

At home, however, there's that familiarity and the dog and owner will often feel more at ease. It's such a horrible situation wherever it happens that the owner or dog are never going to be completely comfortable with what is happening. It is one of those times when, as part of a veterinary team, you hope everything will go well and you try your hardest to make sure it does.

In the end, circumstances and the urgency of the euthanasia often dictate when and where it takes place, and personally I've had animals euthanized at home, in the practice, and even in the back of a car. In Mum's Kerry's case it was at the veterinary clinic. She had been in the theatre for exploratory surgery, and later that day Mum received a phone call to say that Kerry had an inoperable cancer. So she wouldn't suffer, it was better that they didn't let her come around from the operation. And so, without saying goodbye to her, Mum let her go. I sensed she always regretted not having gone into the surgery to say goodbye while Kerry was still asleep and before she was euthanized. This was something offered by the veterinarian when they phoned, but sometimes people can panic and do what's right for everyone at that particular moment, and not necessarily what's right for themselves.

Looking at all those pictures of dogs gone by, and especially when I think about what happened to Kerry, I can't help remembering the first euthanasia I ever assisted with when I was doing my veterinary nursing training. It was 1981 and this dog, too, had been admitted for exploratory surgery and had been found to have cancer which had metastasized. When the owner wept over the loss of her old dog, it was the first time I had ever seen such an open display of grief by someone

I didn't know. It is something I've never forgotten. That afternoon of so long ago is still imprinted in my mind; as clear now as it was back then. There are some things you experience which affect you forever more, and that is one of mine.

A few weeks after Kerry died, we heard of a little toy dog named Skye who was looking for a home. Mum fell in love with that tiny little black and white papillon dog with his fluffy butterfly ears. They immediately bonded with one another and she used to carry him when he wanted to be carried, feed him whatever he wanted to eat, and walk him whenever he wanted to be walked. Like so many tiny toy dogs, there is often little doubt over who is in charge, and it so frequently isn't the human. Not that this matters, though, as long as everyone is happy and benefits from the 'agreement.' Both Mum and Skye certainly seemed very happy with their very own human-canine contract.

Mum's bad luck with dogs was unfortunately not over. She lived in a quiet cul-de-sac opposite a park, and one fateful day she was in there taking Skye for a walk and he was walking off his lead. He suddenly spotted Martin walking towards the park and dashed out of the park to greet him. Before Mum could react, poor little Skye had been run over by a passing car. It was such a sad time. We were all devastated.

Mum thought she would never have another dog as long as she lived. She felt she couldn't bear the heartbreak that she felt each time she lost one. Until the day she died she had Skye's photograph in a silver frame on the mantel piece above the fire. I found that photograph in among her things earlier today. She would occasionally become tearful about him. I think she thought she had failed him; that she should have been able to have done something to have stopped the accident from happening. But accidents happen, and there'd previously been no indication that he wouldn't come back when called—until that point his recall had been sound. It was a park and the area was such a quiet one; I think in the end it was just the most awful bad luck.

A long time ago at a conference on animal euthanasia and human emotions, I heard a wise lady say that when she was still working as a veterinary surgeon in practice, people would often say to her once their dog had been euthanized that they couldn't possibly get another animal because it is so hard to lose them. She would say to them that by not having one they would be denying themselves the love of that animal, and the love that they could give to another being. Why deny yourself that love, and the opportunity to love back? Why miss out on that beneficial reciprocal relationship; that happiness that can be shared? When there are so many animals in need of being loved, and you have a space in your heart and life, why not give another animal a chance to be loved? The happy times will so outweigh the sad ones.

Mum did remain dog-less for several months, and I worried about her a lot during that time. Dogs provide great company, and this was something Mum was desperate for. When she had a dog in her life she had to go out several times a day; during this time she didn't really go out more than a couple of times a week. When people live alone dogs provide a necessary interaction that helps to enrich their lives.

A twist of fate, however, led her to another dog—a dog very different to little Skye.

Gail was a sheepdog. A Border collie used to living in the country and having only the farm cat, the free range chickens, and a multitude of sheep for company. In 2001 foot and mouth disease hit our region and resulted in her flock of sheep being prematurely slaughtered and, well, no sheep meant that she no longer had a job to do. In my mind the matching was immediate, i.e. a dog in need of a human; a human in need of a dog. So I phoned Mum and told her about the displaced collie dog. I have to admit she took a bit of persuading that this could work, but I persisted. She was still of the ilk that she couldn't bear to have to go through all that heartache again. Still, I persisted . . . and then eventually she gave in.

Hence, one evening as the stench of funeral pyres of burning cows and sheep lay heavily on the air, I delivered Gail to her. As far as we knew she had never before been in a pet home, but after a couple of weeks during which she had to get the hang of house-training, Gail quite enthusiastically took to being a pet dog. And so, a pet dog she remained for the rest of her life. She had been five years old when Mum took her in, and fifteen when she died and, on losing her, once again Mum was devastated. The two of them had shared ten years of a reciprocally affectionate friendship. That bond between them made Mum's life much richer than it would have been had she not had Gail there with her.

All these dogs had helped her through some tough times—even Rusty her childhood dog had been there for her and her family during the war. It can't have been easy for any child born at the outbreak of the Second World War, because by the time the war had ended Mum, and children like her, had never known a world without conflict. In the years to come, however, Mum's dogs would help her through times when she could hardly face the day; days when, for her, there seemed to be no hope of ever again being happy.

In return for their affection through the traumas of her life, she would provide those dogs with a loving home, the best dog food she could afford, far too many unsuitable treats, and the best veterinary care.

Those dogs had been there for her; just as she had been there for them; just as she had expected to be there for Lucy. And it had been Gail's leaving this world that paved the way for this feisty little terrier. Dear, sweet, little Lucy.

When Gail passed away, in a desperate bid to not allow Mum enough time to say she couldn't possibly have another dog, I immediately started searching local rescue shelters. Mum insisted that if she were to have another dog, as she herself was much older by then, that dog would have to be small. No other prerequisite, just small and, of course, definitely a rescue dog in need of a forever home—just as all her previous dogs had been

Small dogs often get homes more quickly than larger ones—they're cute, cheaper to keep, generally good to have around children, and you don't need to go and invest in a large car and a house with a big garden. The popularity of these little canines was not helping me to locate a suitable small enough rescue dog.

My friends on social media include many ex-students who now work in rescue so, disappointed that I hadn't been able to find a dog small enough, having a brainwave I posted a message telling the whole world what had happened to Mum's dog Gail. I then went on to carefully describe the type of dog Mum would now like to offer a home to. This was, as all my conversations with Mum had been hypothetical, without her knowing. This is something I would strongly advise others to never do!

Within half an hour, however, there was an image of Lucy underneath my posting. Immediately I got on the phone to Mum and described this little Irish dog to her.

There was no resistance. Perhaps Mum had realized she stood no hope of being successful in refusing to accept that her life was better with a dog in it. Perhaps, and I like to think this was the case, she realized how well she'd fared from her years with Gail and all Gail's predecessors.

And so, Lucy came home.

Mum's only hesitation had been that the dog she gave a home to could possibly outlive her. We all realized that when a person gets old, statistically there's a greater chance the dog may, indeed, outlive the owner. I had always promised Mum that if she had a dog and the dog did just that, then I would have the dog. So before she would take on this little terrier, she insisted I repeat my promise there, then, that if ever anything happened to her, I would indeed have Lucy.

And now here she is inhabiting our home—this small, long-backed, short-legged, dome-shape faced mixed breed. Already she has become a fundamental part of our lives and will be considered in everything we do.

That was the promise I made.

Tuesday May 13th

Together Without Her

Clare

My Aunt Pat has arrived for Mum's funeral. Seeing her getting off the bus down by the riverside a whole host of feelings flooded through my body. This is all too soon—too soon after my uncle's death just over a year ago. His death, too, had been unexpected and here we are with another sudden death in the family. Not just any death: that of my dear mum—Pat's sister.

As we hugged at the bus station, the years melted away. I was suddenly the child and she the adult. She is the wise one who knows what's right to do in these situations; she's the one I can turn to who can solve my worries. The last time we were together was last summer when Bob and I visited Birmingham to catch up with everyone we see only once a year. Almost a whole year ago, yet it feels like it was only yesterday.

There's a multitude of feelings that go on deep inside you on the night before you are going to say a final farewell to your mother; while you are sitting with the dogs curled up beside you, reminiscing with your family about the past. I don't think the true depth of what has happened has yet sunk in. I can't cry. I feel tearful, yes, but proper sobbing, which is what I think I should be doing? That open display of grief just won't come.

Pat is glad to see Lucy. She has never met her before, having only ever heard about her from Mum. While she and I were sitting there earlier, Lucy was by her side and Pat was gently stroking her, caressing her ears and stroking her small head. I wonder whether Lucy senses a familial connection. Lucy doesn't know what's going on—this is all so strange to her. She has been catapulted into a new life, which for now is among people who aren't functioning properly; with dogs who, quite frankly, I'm sure would prefer it if she wasn't here.

Earlier on today I got the food ready for the funeral and loaded it all into the fridge and freezer. It feels strange even thinking that tomorrow is Mum's funeral. Everything: my dealing with the undertaker, choosing songs and hymns for the service, thinking that she is no longer living and breathing, and knowing that I've said all that I will ever say to her—it all feels strangely surreal.

Pat is still in a state of shock, I can tell. She has lost her brother and sister in the space of just more than a year. Eighteen months ago none of us would have imagined that any of this would happen—we were all just bumbling along with our own little worlds; funerals and all that goes with them were the furthest things from our minds.

Having the dogs here is helping. They have a calming influence on us all. They seem to know there's something up and appear to be treading more delicately than usual. There is a sense that they realize things have changed—that things really are not going to be the same again. Do dogs have that sense of future events? I don't know . . . I really don't, but what I do know is that they definitely seem to recognize their lives are different now. Whether they know the permanence of that is a question many generations of people will have considered when pondering the true grasp that animals have of the past, present and future.

Saturday May 17th

After the funeral

Clare

Funeral day was three days ago, and with so few likely to be in attendance, we decided to have the 'wake' back at our house. We considered this carefully, but hoped that if it was a sunny day we could drift into the garden. Amid my need to get everything organized, and in the limited amount of time I had available, I forgot (and how could I possibly have done so), that while we were at the chapel we would need to leave the dogs alone for only the third or fourth time since Lucy arrived. Not only that, but when we returned from the service, the increasing number of people who were, by then, coming along to the funeral, would be milling around the house and garden, eating food (definitely a Peggy-attraction), and having a drink or two.

In the end the day of the funeral was, except for how we were all feeling inside, a beautiful day. When I woke up in the morning, for what felt ages I gazed at the ceiling. I had what has become a familiar hard, jagged rock firmly wedged in the space below my diaphragm. As realization washed over me that this was going to be the day of my mother's funeral, I took the deepest intake of breath, rolled onto my side, and pulled my knees right up to my chest. I wanted to let out a massive wail that has been festering deep inside me. But no sound would come. At this point Lucy, no doubt sensing and perhaps sharing my despair, came up to my face and looked deep into my eyes, willing me to get up. The sun was shining through the gap in the curtains bringing with it a warmth not normally experienced this time of year, this far north. The light cast a band of light across Lucy's face, highlighting what looked like a sense of urgency in her eyes. Like an obedient android, machine not human, I shifted off the bed with my new dog at my side, and got on with whatever path my day would take.

When the time came to leave we gave the dogs their pre-us-leaving-the-house treats. Ralph took them gently and then pushed them around on the floor before eating them, in the way which we've become accustomed to seeing him do. As was her reluctant wont (she would prefer to snatch them out of your hand and run off with them, but has been trained not to do this), Peggy was polite, also taking them gently. Lucy, obviously originating from the Peggy school of dog training, snatched them but then spat them out on the floor. She then immediately began to run around us, barking. She knew we were going out and I suppose she sensed it was going to be somewhat of an emotional outing. Dogs know—somehow, they know.

We were only twelve days into our adventure with Lucy; just twelve days since my mum (and hers) had left us orphaned. She was stressed, we were stressed, and

Peggy and Ralph, picking up on the anxious vibes, were I'm sure, wondering what on Earth had happened to their peaceful existence.

Knowing that timing was critical, in that way he has which I wish I had, before we left the house Anthony spent a few minutes calming the dogs. Meanwhile, the rest of us headed out to the car to wait for him.

The chapel is beside a beautifully calm, man-made lake. Both the lake and the chapel are surrounded by trees and the new leaves were gently whispering in the breeze. We could hear the birds who have made the area their home chirruping away to themselves or any other birds who would stop by to listen to their conversations. There was a pair of swans swimming along the water's edge with their beige-feathered, fluffy cygnet swimming between them.

Throughout the service we could see those elegant swans as they went about their peaceful business, gliding along beside some mallards and a coot that had popped along for a splash in the sun-kissed water. If we could have paid a fortune for a more fitting 'send-off', then this was what we would have ordered. But days like that and scenes like that happen by chance and can't be bought, and we are all thankful that the memory of Mum's farewell is wrapped up in that scene.

Inside the chapel we listened to Mum's eulogy and songs and hymns we had chosen for her. One was Doris

Day singing *Que sera, sera*; something we chose because of Mum's life-long love of Doris. The other was a song whose title we found on a piece of paper when we were sorting out her things. The message was written in Mum's unmistakable, clear, careful handwriting and was entitled 'Funeral Song'. Underneath the definitively instructive title, it said Westlife: *You Raise Me Up.*

A few days before the funeral I sat on the sofa with the piece of paper in hand. The dogs were curled up around me and I played the song over and over again on the laptop. I could imagine her seeing it once or twice on the television and how she would have carefully absorbed the words and how, perhaps, it would have made her cry. I don't know when she wrote the message, but I felt glad we had found the piece of paper before the funeral. For all those years Mum had never mentioned it; never mentioned that she was a closet Westlife fan! I had heard the song on the radio, but had never really properly listened to it. There had been no hesitation in our choosing Doris Day, but we had struggled with knowing which other one to choose—Mum's scribbled piece of paper that we found among her masses of paperwork provided such a welcome answer.

Leaving the chapel with a convoy of vehicles behind us, a by then familiar feeling of dread entered the pit of my stomach: *'All these people were coming back to our house and it could be in dog-induced chaos!'* Perhaps I hadn't thought it through properly? Perhaps I should have hired a small venue instead of putting the dogs and us through all this stress?

Arriving back home, very gingerly, we opened the front door. Peggy was doing vertical jumps (something she's been trained not to do), but with a quick, 'Find a toy, Peggy', off she went to find a toy, dutifully coming back in a much calmer state with the toy firmly wedged between her jaws. Her bottom was waggling in her wake, demonstrating her desperate keenness to greet 'the visitors'. Peggy knows that having visitors usually means being given treats!

Ralph kept back from all the commotion, watching and waiting to see what was going on. Lucy, having long-ago mastered the art of Peggy-like vertical jumps, leaped up and down, but her leaps were not so dangerous due to the very obvious size difference between her and Peggy—Peggy being a long, tall greyhound, and Lucy only a quarter of the size. And so, she got away with it. I suppose this supports the theory that has been proven time and time again—small dogs get away with things that large dogs never do.

As we made our way into the kitchen, scanning for any damage done to furniture, plants, carpets or house, Lucy seemed unconcerned about the puddle of urine she'd left on the kitchen rug. 'Don't let anyone in!' Bob screeched back at me, as he reached for the under-sink cupboard door and the cleaning equipment secured inside. He was obviously more concerned about Lucy's misdemeanour than Lucy seemed to be. She was keen to investigate the people who were waiting outside, rather than worrying about a measly, unimportant puddle of urine on the rug.

Dutifully barring the front door so no one could get in until the floor was mopped, I stalled for time, showing everyone the spring flowers in the rockery, and marveling at the beautiful sunshiny day. Something was carrying me through. The person moving around and speaking to people was not me. Inside, my world had just broken, and this was some dreamlike existence beyond the life in which I had existed until just two weeks earlier.

Once scrubbed, the purple rug had a one and a half feet diameter dark stain right across its middle. When we were all 'allowed' in the house, everyone immediately headed for the kitchen and we warned them all about the damp patch: 'Mind the wet patch, right there in the middle of the rug—and please don't take off your shoes,' we told them over and over as we danced around them trying to guide their forty or fifty feet around the aforementioned damp area. It wasn't that they couldn't see it, more that they didn't seem as bothered about it as we were!

The beautiful, sun-drizzled afternoon progressed without event. We were careful—Lucy was attached to one of us by a lead because we are not yet completely confident that her dog aggression doesn't extend to people. The other two canines milled around the people, while the people milled around them and each other. The food we'd put up high and out of the way earlier that morning was distributed, and samosas and onion bhajis (Mum's favourites) put in the oven to warm. Their pungent curry aroma mingled with the garlic bread. These spicy smells filled the house with their scents, resulting in a weird environmental perfume of garlic curry combined with lavender polish, due to the obsessive cleaning I'd done in the previous few days.

Amid the crowd, nervous Ralph managed to find himself his very own dog whisperer in the form of Pete, one of my brother's friends. Paul (quite impressively, I might add), reached forward and stroked Ralph without him having that normal (normal for Ralph anyway) recoil he does when he isn't expecting a hand to reach out towards him. Strangely, Ralph dutifully responded in a way in which your average friendly dog would, rather than the nervous dog he is. Perhaps the cat-loving Pete missed his true vocation, and a dog whisperer he should have been?

Ralph is funny though. Not funny-ha-ha, but funny-strange. He really is extremely worried about people—especially when we are out for walks. In a situation like Mum's funeral when there are a lot of people about, however, he stays right there in the hub of everyone and doesn't go off and hide away. I don't know whether it has something to do with sensory overload, in that he gets himself into a situation whereby people drift towards him and then he feels he can't move, but it is strange that when he is given the opportunity to move, he just stays where he is on the sofa, chair, or dog bed on which he has positioned himself. The whole time he steadfastly watches everyone. Perhaps it is his version of keeping his enemies close?

There's a dog a colleague sometimes brings into work. He's called Sammi and he's a black Labrador. Being a black Lab, he's obviously nothing like Ralph to look at, but there's a glint in his eye that is just like a playful spark I occasionally see in Ralph. I feel sad that, given a different start in life, Ralph could have been that bold, confident dog just like Sammi.

The dogs are confused with all the coming and going, but by the weekend things will hopefully settle down. Next week there will be a greater sense of normality as I'll be back at work and there will be a familiar structure to our lives—familiar for us, though, not so for Lucy. At least for the time being Anthony is here, which makes everything less worrying as he will be around to look after the dogs. Although I don't think that will stop me from worrying about them all—especially little Lou!

Monday May 19th

Normal with Something Missing and Something Extra

Clare

I returned to work today. Very quickly it seems as though I've not been away and life has already resumed a sense of routine. The students are approaching one of their busiest times of the year and my absence has eaten into the time I would have had with them. Keeping busy today and catching up with what they need from me has helped to keep me distracted.

There has been a gaping hole in the pit of my stomach each time I think of telling Mum something, and then remember for the umpteenth time I can never do that again—not unless I speak to the air in front of me, which I have found myself doing from time to time. Like this morning, for instance, when I was out in the garden wandering around checking on how the blossom is coming along on the fruit trees and Lucy was attached to my heels in that way she seems attuned to; those are the times when I can speak out loud and make out that I am talking to one of the dogs.

The three dogs are helping me so much. Dogs don't judge or question anything you say or do. I am finding that one of them is always attached to my side; almost as though they are on some guarding rota they have established all by themselves. All the time they are here being supportive and hanging on closely to my every word. And that is helping—it is helping me a lot.

Before I walked into the office today I took a huge deep breath and then opened the door. With hugs all around, I managed to hold back the tears. Not that the tears have properly come—I feel I don't know what to expect. I guess I simply don't know how I *should* be.

I phoned home at lunch time to check up on the dog politics with Anthony. All was going well. Poor little Lucy—three years she had spent with Mum, and here she is, catapulted into a world with a very different routine from the one to which she had become accustomed. She has a desire to protect everyone from, well, anything that may be considered a threat. This especially, at the moment anyway, very much applies to Ralph and Peggy. Lucy seems intent on defending us from their wrath, or what she perceives to be their wrath, which usually just means that they want to come and sit beside one of us.

Lucy's history is vague because Mum got her from the rescue centre. All we know is that she had been living in Northern Ireland as a stray, and had perhaps been used for breeding. With no space for her in the rescue homes in Northern Ireland, she was brought over on the boat to Scotland. Just like with Ralph, who was brought up here from England, our local kennels does this whenever they have a space in order to help ease the stray problem in areas beyond our region.

It was a few years ago when we first went with Mum to collect Lucy. Mum hadn't been at all perturbed by the screeching coming from behind the door as the kennel assistant carried Lucy through to where we were waiting. This was our second visit to the kennels, and Mum was already smitten. 'Oh look, here she is!' Mum declared as she reached forward to caress the ears of this little dog with a big attitude. Meanwhile, I had flashbacks to all those similar snappy little dogs with bared teeth who'd demonstrated such attitudes when I was working as a nurse in veterinary practice. 'Isn't she sweet?' Mum asked in a quite rhetorical manner. And all I could do was nod.

Lucy *is* sweet. She has a 'soft' look, which is when she relaxes her ears and looks calm and peaceful; her 'harsh' look is much angrier altogether, and this is when anyone around has to be on their guard. She is affectionate too, selectively, but nevertheless affectionate. She's not dangerous, she's just a dog you need to sometimes be careful interacting with. She's the kind of dog you need to warn your vet about when you lift her onto the consulting room table.

When she was still living her life as Mum's protector, I used to sometimes have difficulty when clipping her nails, but today I discovered that if I catch her when she's relaxed she lets me do it without her reacting in that Lucy-terrier way. I think, perhaps, that Mum's presence in that situation made Lucy worse, as Lucy always felt she had to defend Mum, and whenever I was manipulating toes and nail clippers, Lucy was unable to fulfill her duty as resident guard dog.

As a family we've become accustomed to lurchers and greyhounds and their gentle, calm ways. You don't need to try too hard with sight hounds—they just love to be in your company and are happy, well, to just 'be'. Terriers and terrier types, however, are renowned for their eagerness and keenness to protect and to be into everything. They are such busy dogs; it's as though they constantly need to know what's going on—and Lucy is no exception.

You definitely need to be one step ahead of her, and earlier this evening when I was in the kitchen cooking the dinner, Ralph popped out into the garden to go to the toilet. Having done his business, he was happily trotting through the back door ready to head towards his much-loved chair. Upon seeing him coming into the kitchen, Lucy chased him out of the house, growling and snarling. This has confirmed for me, more than ever, that we have our hands full, and that keeping that aforementioned one step ahead of her is going to be somewhat of a challenge.

Lucy can sometimes be such a little bully!

Sunday May 25th

Grey Hair, Grey Faces

Clare

It's my birthday, and naturally I don't feel like celebrating. When does the grey hair suddenly appear, though? One gene I inherited which turned out to be not such a bad one, was the one which blessed me with hair which, now on my 49th birthday, I still don't need to dye or, indeed, to consider making the decision to gracefully go grey.

Just a few days ago, however, we were invited to go for a meal at a friend's house—a nice meal and a chance to offload. So, there I was getting ready to go out, and there *it* was—a coarse, thick, pure white hair sticking out of the top of my head. Without a second thought, I reached up, plucked it from its root, and marched through to Bob to show him the evidence of my ageing. 'Oh, that?' he proclaimed, 'that's been there for a while . . . there are some more as well.'

My indignant declarations that he should have informed me of this fact were met with a shrug. As I glanced at the half-grey, half-black locks atop his own head, perhaps I understood why he hadn't bothered.

Like ageing creeps up on us humans, so too, it does our dogs. Just days ago I noticed poor old Ralph, still only just approaching his middle age, had grey patches appearing like shadows across his face. I noticed Peggy, too, a little more mature, had developed distinguished-looking 'I know all there is to know about these humans,' grey eyebrows appearing above her velvet-brown eyes, and there is now more white than black on her muzzle. Being blessed with a white muzzle anyway, Lucy will take much longer to show those same visible signs of getting old, but even she is beginning to develop the tell-tale opacity of cataracts developing in both eyes.

Mum was seventy-four when she died. She was very nearly seventy-five, at which age she was very excited about going to at last be in receipt of a free TV license. Even at that age she had never became fully-grey. Like many people she used to dye her hair from time to time, but on the occasions when she let her natural dark brunette hair peek through, she still had some dark hairs lingering in the grey and white shadows of her aged crown.

Mum was no different to anyone else who suddenly finds themselves beyond their three score years and ten and who wonders where those years have gone. As she approached the time when her life would so suddenly come to an end, she said that time seemed like only a whisper from the days when she was the young, carefree woman working for Cadbury. While the skin on her arms had become like fragile, delicate, thin tissue paper that looked as though it might tear if it caught on a sharp thorn on the roses she tended, her face was smooth and glowing. It seemed that, along with her hair, her face had also defied her age. While her arms could be hidden by sleeves, the combination of her face and her hair lied, and made people believe she was much younger than she appeared to be. In the latter years she used to say she wished she looked older than she did, so that people would realize there were things she was no longer capable of physically doing—things like lifting Lucy into a car or onto the weighing scales at the veterinary clinic.

As she got older, Mum's age was instead more obviously displayed in the creaking of her joints and her slow, deliberate movements as we made our way around the supermarket each Sunday afternoon. While we went off on this weekly excursion, Lucy would be waiting back at the flat, on guard on the back of the sofa so she could see out of the window—the little dog bravely defending all her person's worldly goods. Even when it was cool and it would have been okay for us to have taken Lucy in the car to the supermarket, we didn't. This was because any enforced separation from Mum was something Lucy couldn't bear, and she would screech and howl from the back of the car. She was not even a little consoled if any of the rest of us—people she knew well—were sitting with her. I tried it a few times and, as we sat in the car parked outside the chemist, even though she could actually see Mum waiting at the counter, she would bark, whine, and howl at the top of her little terrier voice. Lucy would continue this shrieking until Mum was safely back in the car, at which point she would leap about in sheer delight.

I was in the supermarket with Mum and Martin just six days before she died. Mum showed no signs of dying; no signs that that would be the last time we would deliberate over what to take back with us to make for our late Sunday lunch. There was no warning that this would be the final time the three of us would walk together along the supermarket aisles. Each time we would finish up at the pet food section, where Mum would carefully decide which type of food she would take home as her latest offerings to Lucy; lest she offend this little dog with something she did not find acceptable!

Speaking of Lucy, I imagine it's about time we heard a little of what might be going on in her crazy little terrier head . . .

Saturday June 7th

Lucy Has Her Say

Lucy

Lucy-Luella is my name—just Lucy to my friends. They say I'm a mixture-dog, a bits-of-everything dog, a crossbreed, a mongrel—some even say I'm a 'Heinz 57', whatever one of those is! It would seem that my genes are mostly Jack Russell terrier, with a bit of Chihuahua and a bit of corgi thrown in. Like I said, I'm a bits-of dog.

What appears to be common to the breeds that have created me is that they all have extremely short legs. You'd think this would matter—especially when you consider I live with two large dogs, both of whom are three times my height. But size doesn't matter in dog-politics when you consider the genetic advantages my 'bits-of' genetic heritage has gifted me.

Those big dogs are not very inquisitive, and would rather be lazing around on the sofa with their legs in the air than doing anything important. That terrier part of me makes me desperate to check out what the humans are doing. When we go for a walk, it's always yours truly who keeps the local dog population in order by emitting low grumbling growls from the back of my throat, baring my teeth, threatening them with my stare, and raising those hairs along my back. That makes me look larger but, like I said, size doesn't matter.

We have toys around the house and those two big dogs know which ones are mine and wouldn't DARE touch them. I've allocated which ones they are allowed to have and that keeps the peace. They may be larger than I am, but they know who's in charge. If they get too excited when we play in the garden, for instance, I chase them straight back inside—I'll have none of that nonsense going on around me. And then, when it's feeding time . . . hmm . . .

Ah, yes, feeding time, well, this is perhaps the only time that I have just a minor disadvantage. The disadvantage, I'm afraid to say, is that of a lack of height. The other two, being the types of tall, long-legged dogs that can get that twisted stomach thing, have to eat from bowls which are on very high stands in order to stop them from gulping down too much air. Unfortunately, try as I may, however much I extend my neck and try to stretch my legs to make myself taller, I just can't reach their food. This is when the two of them give me those apparently-invisible-to-humans smug, sidelong glances, and I have to admit defeat and eat my own paltry-sized portion.

I suppose there are, indeed, times when size *does* matter . . . however much we little ones try.

Anyway, we'll leave that minor issue for now and get back to the matter in hand, and how I ended up living here with these two sofa-hogging hounds.

Well, don't you just know that the old woman left me? One day she was there, and the next there was all this kerfuffle (a word I often used to hear her say), and I suddenly found myself sitting in the vehicle with the one who was always with those two dogs—stupid Ralph and that Peggy-one with the pointed face who always tries to steal my toys. Everyone was a bit quiet in the vehicle, so I whined a bit for some attention. Why were they taking me away from the place with the old woman and the big green space where I kept all the other dogs in check?

I had been a bit concerned about the old woman. She hadn't been too well and I tried to lick her to make her feel better, but she seemed much worse than I'd seen her before. I howled to get her to speak to me, but she wouldn't. And then, in the morning when the one arrived who would always come to take me to the green space where the dogs were, I barked and barked at the window to get him to come and help, but it took ages for him to get in. When eventually he managed to get inside there were strangers with him, so I darted through to the bedroom to protect the old woman from them. What else could I do? In the end, though, I let him attach my lead and take me out of the room. All the time I pulled to get back, but eventually I had to give in.

Shortly after this, Ralph's people arrived and I positioned myself next to Ralph's person while she communicated with a man in dark clothes.

And then, well, after a few very fraught hours followed by a journey with Ralph's people, I ended up here in this house, being forced to be in the company of the aforementioned Ralph and Peggy.

Peggy. Ah yes, Peggy. I've already mentioned how she has a tendency to steal my toys. You'd never understand why, though, because she has heaps of her own all to herself. And I do mean heaps! The strange thing is that she carries them around in her mouth. I have a vague recollection of being carried around like that when I was just a pup, but I think that she, that Peggy, believes those stuffed creatures are actually puppies.

She also does this bizarre thing with her toys when we can hear the people coming home. As soon as they're just outside the door or we can hear them coming down the path, she picks up one of her toys and dances around with it in her mouth. I have never seen anything quite so ridiculous. She does the same whenever visitors come to the house. She is a very weird dog.

I noticed some time ago that she has quite large teeth so I thought it might be a good idea, solely in the interests of my long-term survival strategy of course, to pretend to be one of those puppies. With this in mind, one day I stood beside her and reached up and licked her mouth. That's apparently what those young canines would do back in the days of our great ancestors, the wolf. I thought it would protect my general wellbeing.

And, do you know what? She was fooled—I felt quite vindicated in my submissive actions when I realized she's just as stupid as that silly clot Ralph. Puppies do it so their parents will feed them, but I didn't really want her to regurgitate any food. Gosh, no, that would have been disgusting, and quite embarrassing at my age. No, I did it just enough to protect me from her wrath. I didn't know for sure whether she had any wrath, or even precisely what wrath was, but I wasn't going to risk finding out.

I had been here a few days and a few nights, or maybe more, I can't really tell for sure as the days all seem to be the same. Anyway, Ralph's person and the rest of them had all been away for a while and I got a bit excited when I heard them coming back with a lot of other people, and so I peed on the floor. When Ralph's people came in, the man got some stuff that didn't smell very nice and rubbed it into where I had peed. He was really fussing over it, so I left him to it. Meanwhile, Ralph's person went outside and it seemed to be a long time before they all came into the house. I have to say, the kitchen rug smelt revolting of whatever he had put on it. It smelt much better how I had left it.

For some reason I was put on a lead and only had restricted access to all the nice people; while Ralph and Peggy did what they wanted. I really don't think that was very fair. I was quite relieved when eventually all the visitors went away and I was given back my freedom.

A lady stayed here for a few nights around that time—she reminded me of the old woman. I wonder where the old woman has gone to and when she will come back and collect me.

Thursday June 26th

Animals Losing Animals; Animals Losing People

Clare

It is my kidney birthday today. It is twelve years since Bob gave me his kidney. I still sometimes have to stop and think about the utterly altruistic way in which he did this. There was never any hesitation on his behalf regarding what he was going to have to go through—it was just something he was desperate to do to make me and our small family better again. The time has flown, and amid all this current heartache I have to remember how very lucky I am. I look around me and I know, I really do see how fortunate I am, but there are times when other emotions can take a hold of you and cast a shadow over everything else. For now the time is for us to mourn, but also be thankful for what we have. And just now for us, mixed up in the loss of Mum, there's the added worry of having a very bereft dog in our midst.

When I think of Lucy's situation it makes me think of many of the dogs I've come across over the years who haven't been as lucky as she has been. Through my work over the past three and a half decades, I've seen and heard of so many dogs going into rescue when their owner passes away. In many of these situations there has been a lot of heart-wrenching discussion and soul-searching on behalf of the relatives. This is usually because they had not ever imagined wanting a dog of their own and had built their life as one which is dog-free. A dog is a huge undertaking—they really do change your whole world, and you can perhaps see why some people realize their lifestyle is not going to suit that of the dog. In a no-kill shelter, hopefully the dog will find their way towards a new, loving home; or preferably some relatives will hold onto their loved one's animal until they can find a good home for them where they can check in on them from time to time.

The cases that have been extremely upsetting, though, have been those where the bereft dog has become an inconvenience and, quite frankly, the family members of the deceased person don't care. I know people express their grief in many different ways, and what you see in front of you is often not a true reflection of that person or how they are feeling, but when no one phones to see how the dog is getting along . . . that can be hard to deal with when you're working in rescue. That creature who had been cherished by their loved one is sometimes banished into rescue (or euthanized) without a second thought. And that is incredibly sad.

On the day Mum died we were never asked by the police what was going to happen to Lucy: this petrified little creature who was pushing herself into my side, and who was watching the policeman's every move. Before the policeman left I asked whether he needed to know what was going to happen to her, but this was not apparently included in the 'sudden death of a citizen' paperwork. Even in my confused, bereft state, I couldn't help thinking how bizarre it was that that should be the case! Perhaps the police officer would normally have asked just out of a sense of public responsibility, so if necessary he could have alerted an animal welfare charity. The issue of people's animals is surely something important which exists beyond the remit of a piece of paper. It's possible he sensed, however, that we would be taking her home with us and simply didn't feel it necessary to delve deeper? Perhaps he could see we all genuinely cared for this crazy little mixed up dog.

Do animals *truly* understand what has happened when someone passes away? I imagine the main evidence we have is in how they behave when it happens. It is certainly the case that many animals appear to express signs which indicate they are feeling out of sorts when someone dies. But perhaps the term 'out of sorts' is not an intense enough reflection of how they behave; somehow it doesn't properly describe the utter despair shown by some animals when they lose someone they love.

We know for sure that for Lucy the permanent separation from Mum has been a huge thing—as it is for any dog whose human companion passes away. Dogs really do appear to show signs of grief, and this sense of loss is expressed in the ways in which they behave when they lose someone. The signs they show are precisely those that we humans experience. They will sigh a lot and search for their lost loved one; they may go off their food and become withdrawn and lethargic; some may become more attached to someone else or another animal; and the dynamics in a multi-pet household can often completely shift. Some may also develop behavioural problems such as aggression towards one another, and others may develop toilet training issues.

Just as people do, animals in the same household may respond in different ways to losing a person or another animal companion. Years ago, our old and very poorly black and brindle crossed collie Fluke was euthanized at home, and at the time we had two other dogs—Jack and Oskar. Jack showed most of the signs of loss I've described above. It was awful for him, and we desperately tried to distract him and keep him busy. The bond between him and Fluke had been such a strong one, and Fluke's loss made him incredibly sad. I remember reading in the time leading up to Fluke's euthanasia that it helps once the euthanasia is over to let the other animals in the house see their friend once they have passed away. We did this, but I'm not sure with Jack whether it helped one way or the other.

Oskar's reaction to losing Fluke was completely different to Jack's. This was to the extent that, as Bob created a collie-sized hole in the garden in preparation for our ritual, sorrowful farewell to our long-time canine friend, Oskar decided he should give Bob a helping hand! And so, the hole in the ground was ready a bit faster than we had expected, as enthusiastic Oskar's paws raked at that hole as though he was trying to dig his way to Australia. While one dog expressed such sorrowful grief, it was quite clear that the other was not bothered at all about the loss of their old collie companion.

Lucy's main demonstrations of grief have been in how she has become much clingier than she had even been with Mum. She has been exhibiting all the signs similar to those Jack showed on losing Fluke. She has also had this almost insatiable need to check up on me while I am sleeping. It seems as though her memory of being there with Mum when she died is still very strong. As Lucy had so dutifully protected Mum, it appears she feels the need to protect me. She clambers onto the bed and is not happy until she reaches my face and licks me on the cheek, or until I speak to her and gently stroke the soft fur on her small head.

There are many examples across the animal kingdom of animals grieving animals. Apes, dolphins and other cetaceans, elephants, wild dogs, big cats, many bird species, horses, cattle, sheep and other herding animals—it's not difficult to find evidence of all of these and others. This grief extends to relationships that have existed between species—in a domestic setting this is so often seen when dogs lose cats, and vice versa. As time passes we humans are gradually becoming more aware of animals' emotions, however it feels as if we still have a very long way to go in terms of our true appreciation of animals and their feelings.

Meanwhile, we humans express our grief in such diverse ways. The suggested stages of grief: denial, anger, bargaining, depression, acceptance—all of these stages, well, I guess they have become a mantra for how I should be feeling. Should I be angry? If so, how and when should I express that anger? Should I be depressed? Or should I accept what has happened and just get on with my life? But grief doesn't seem to be like that. Just like in animals, it doesn't appear to follow a one size fits all pattern.

Clare Cogbill

Saturday July 12th

Getting Along With 'The Others'

Lucy

The food around here is no dog's dinner, I can tell you! I suppose I should clarify that—it IS a dog's dinner, and that's precisely where the problem lies. The old woman, you see, while she did actually give me some of that revolting food for dogs, she didn't really expect me to eat it! Of course she didn't! Why would I want to eat that if I was quite happy eating the slices of meat she bought especially for me? She didn't eat them herself, she'd given up eating animals before I came on the scene, but she was quite happy to buy these tasty slices for me. I used to sense that Ralph's person was a bit angry about the old woman feeding them to me, saying something about how they were not good for humans, so why would they be good for dogs? But the old woman never stopped doing it. As you'd probably expect, there's none of that tasty stuff around here!

Ralph and Peggy get all excited and pathetic about this awful stuff you have to crunch, when really it's far too much effort to eat. For a while I starved myself in protest at the revulsion of it all. Eventually, however, and extremely surprisingly for me, I gave in. It appears that the will of Ralph and Peggy's people is far greater than my own!

Well, I've got to eat something!

Anyway, getting back to Peggy and Ralph. Once I had mastered the submissive 'feed-me', licking of the mouth thing with Peggy, I decided to revert to my old ways of keeping them both in order!

I first of all set out on a mission to let Ralph know that he's only allowed to use the back door when I say so. What this means is that if we all go out into the garden to play or go to the toilet, I have to make sure I'm back in the house first, just so I can chase him back outside when he tries to come in! There isn't any real purpose to this, except to cause a little trouble and let him know I'm now in charge of things around here.

It really is the best of fun! Or should I say it *was* fun, until the people stopped me from doing it. Can you believe it? They actually put me through the other kitchen door into the hallway so that Ralph was able to come back into the house without my say so! It would seem they are intent on 'training' me! Once that part of the dog training strategy was complete (although I have to say that personally I wouldn't really call it training because I had no choice in the matter. I couldn't chase him if the door was closed and I couldn't actually see what was happening!), they did allow me to remain in the kitchen while he came back in. This was really not fair game though, because they held on to me over on the far side of the room while he came through the door.

In Ralph flounced, all triumphant and flapping his big ears and wagging his tail, and following it up with a victorious shake. Meanwhile, I tried to wriggle out of their grasp so I could chase him out of the house but, try as I might, it would seem they are much stronger than I am.

I thought that was the 'training' over and done with, but once I had complied and stopped wriggling, whenever he was coming back into the house, they began to let me go loose. Now instead of holding me they tried to distract me with my favourite toy while he made his way through the back door. I can't believe they really thought that was going to work; of course I immediately ignored the toy and chased him back outside.

Seemingly that wasn't the end of said 'training', and instead once again they kept me over on the far side of the room and held a treat in front of me while I allowed Ralph to come in. That worked, as I'm a little like pointy-faced Peggy in appreciating their offerings. Now I only sometimes chase him. I think he is getting to quite like it, though, which was never my intention. This has sort of taken the fun out of it.

These days the treat for not chasing him only comes occasionally, which in my opinion is actually a bit of a swindle. Apparently it's all part of some random reward strategy people have concocted which works because the dog never really knows for sure whether the treat is coming or not, so we do whatever they want us to do anyway. I have to say, though, I think it's just a scheme they've created so they don't have to fork out for too many treats! I absolutely maintain that it's simply very unjust not to give a treat every time. I still carry out whatever ridiculous nonsense I have to, though, just in case there is actually a morsel coming my way.

Going back to that Peggy one, I have to admit she's a bit more of a challenge to me than Ralph is. She has this aloof look when I try and communicate with her. This is when she gives me a sidelong glance, tosses her long, pointed head, and marches off in another direction with her nose in the air. I really can't quite figure her out, and that is very frustrating for a little dog such as me. I mean, what's with her and all that snootiness? Anyone would think she had some sort of pedigree, and we'll have none of that elite, privileged behaviour around here. It is so unnecessary.

That tossing of the head thing, I've seen Ralph do it too. He does it at cats or those creatures with the very long ears if they happen to be around when we're out on our walks. He never does it at me though. He wouldn't dare! When I want his attention all I have to do is walk underneath him; however that does serve to highlight our obvious size difference, so it's not really the best strategy. The other thing I do is to stand right in front of him and glare at him, at which point he generally gets the idea that he's in my way, or doing something I don't approve of, such as eating food from his own bowl. If he's being particularly annoying, I make a noise in my throat, which absolutely tells him he'd better shift out of my way! He appears to be ignoring me more frequently, though, and I am worried he may be taking lessons from Peggy.

I must say that I am not always as bossy as I could be with Ralph. I do sometimes allow him to get away with things. Those times are mainly when I feel a little off-colour. This sometimes happens when I've been in a deep sleep and I am just waking up and wondering where I am. Those are the times when I think about the old woman and wonder where she is. That's also when I appreciate a little quiet Lucy-time.

There are times when I think I hear the old woman and I look around me, and then I realize it is Ralph's person who has spoken. I look at her and cock my head on one side to make sure. When I realize she's not the old woman I get a strange ache in my chest. Ralph's person usually notices, crouches down next to me and strokes my head. That helps a little, but I do miss the old woman. I miss her a lot.

I think about the times when she and I used to sit quietly, and I would feel her hand gently stroking my neck. I think of the times when she used to let me play ball in the living room, and the times when she would let me select which treat I wanted from the treat bag that used to hang on the door handle in the kitchen. I still get all those things here, but I have to share these people and the treats with the other two.

Friday July 25th

Summer Blues

Clare

I've been off work for a few weeks on summer leave and the three dogs are providing lots of emotional support. Their presence is giving me moments of quiet tranquility to aid in my healing. I hope my being here at home is also helping Lucy. Losing Mum has been such a huge upheaval for this little dog.

Bob and Anthony keep putting films in the DVD player for us all to watch. Even during this the dogs are there, one with their head on my lap; the other two draped one each beside Bob or Anthony. Whichever dog is lying next to me offers their calming, rhythmic breaths and comforting warmth as I stroke their head and back; soothing them, as they in return soothe me.

Ralph is not a head on lap kind of dog—he prefers to lie next to you and nudge his head behind you into the curve of your spine. His warm breath against your clothes can feel like a personal radiator. I think he feels secure like that. It's as though when he has that closeness he is able to escape from all his nervous ways and just be; just exist in the familiarity and security of our reciprocal human-animal bond. Knowing how far he has come on his journey, knowing that he suffered and is now safe, knowing that he can just exist and be happy in our company, all of that is worth so much to us. At times like now when I am in need of his help, he pays me back a thousand times over. This is something he's never needed to do, but which I appreciate with my whole heart.

In recent times it's been discovered that the hormone oxytocin is released whenever we experience closeness with our dogs. Oxytocin is a hormone which is produced in the hypothalamus of the brain and then released by the pituitary gland. It's the same hormone that causes the uterus to contract during childbirth and which is released during breastfeeding. The fact that we release increased levels of this hormone when we are stroking our dogs is perhaps no surprise to dog lovers across the world, nor that the hormone is increasingly becoming known as the nurturing hormone. What may surprise some, however, is that it's now known that dogs do exactly the same when they have close, calm contact with people; when we release oxytocin—so do they.

Our dogs definitely appear to enjoy that mutual contact, and looking around at the positive, calming effects dogs have had on friends' lives, and on the lives of the owners of dogs I have worked with, this same reciprocal, loving relationship is played out time and time again.

While my exterior is calm, however, some kind of front I have applied to make out that everything is okay; on the inside my life has become shrouded in distraction and a sense of utter hopelessness.

So far over the summer when I should have been resting in preparation for the next intake of students, practically every waking moment has been filled with doing something. It doesn't matter what that something is, only that doing that something prevents me from allowing myself to think about Mum. When I sense my mind is drifting towards her, or my eyes are glancing in the direction of her photograph, I switch my thoughts or avert my eyes.

I have nearly finished writing *A Soldier Like Jack*—it was almost completed when Mum died. She had read a first (and very rough) draft before she passed away, and because she is suddenly no longer here, my mission to get it completed has become an obsession. The book is about her grandparents—I was writing it for her. I have to get it finished—even though she will never see the completed manuscript. She will never see her grandfather, Jack, looking out from the cover of the book. I guess with every death there is unfinished business—something significant that was happening that needed to be completed. For her, this is one of those things. She was excited about it, and it makes me very sad that she will never see it come to fruition.

Life has somehow spiraled into a strange kind of overdrive, and sleep has become my only escape, although actually getting to sleep is so difficult. In an effort to force sleep to come, I stay awake as long as I can so it will come more easily; but even then the waking hours of the night are filled with jolts of terror. I think I've become frightened of sleeping—frightened in case I don't wake up. And then when exhaustion has forced slumber, I wake up in the middle of the night, and the dread of the darkness can only be eased by listening to Bob and the dogs' rhythmic breathing.

I mechanically read books at bedtime, never truly taking in the words. I desperately want to find some way of escaping from the nightmare, but I don't entirely trust that someone else's words will provide that necessary distraction. Sometimes what they say even reminds me of what is happening—perhaps a reference to the character's own still-living, still-breathing parents, or some side story about a dog that is lost and alone. And so I read with only part of my mind on the words. Each morning my initial waking moments are accompanied by a tight, hard knot in the depths of my abdomen, and there's a swollen lump sticking in the back of my throat. And I feel exhausted.

The house of the night has become the house of absolute fear, and the morning pit of my stomach has become an aching, gaping hole.

This frantic, incessant overdrive has not gone unnoticed and just today, Bob and Anthony, separately but both with the same degree of concern, told me to slow down—just take stock and relax. They've both told me I am going to burn myself out.

When evening falls, the continuous supply of movies does help a little, providing silver screen therapy in our sitting room. Like the books, however, while this is an opportunity for me to think about something else—at times I feel it's also time to brood as I gaze at the people in those moving pictures on the widescreen TV, and wonder why I am watching; I wonder what time has to offer ordinary people when the people on the screen have been immortalized, and Mum has not.

With interesting films I can sometimes get caught up in the narrative, and for that hour and a half or more there really is true escapism—and then the credits come up and the now familiar knot returns to my gut with a vengeance. For the most part, though, the film plays in the corner of the room, while I became detached and politely wait for it to end. My consolation from all of this is that I am here, with the two people I care most about in the world, and my three dogs. I know I am lucky to have them all. I know they are all dealing with their own grief and the shift in our circumstances, but something deep inside prevents me from being happy.

Sunday July 27th

On Lucy

Ralph

It appears that the little dog with the teeth has come to stay. At first I thought she'd be here for a short while and then leave again like she always used to, but she's still here.

When she first arrived she seemed distant and was very quiet; just not her usual self. Now, though, she's shown that she hasn't become less bossy! For a while I even had to brace myself before I entered the house—even if I'd only been outside to relieve myself up against the bushes or trees in the garden. What she would do is to come outside at the same time as Peggy and me. Peggy would always go back into the house first, mainly because she doesn't like to expend too much energy if she doesn't have to. Then, once Lucy (which is apparently what she is called), had her girly pee—the type of pee that she and Peggy appear to do (although Peggy has been known to lift her leg like I do from time to time, which is very odd), Lucy would race back in the house and wait for me.

Then, as I approached the back door, she would come racing back out, flashing those small, white, needle teeth at me. The first few times she did it I was petrified and I started to go around to the other back door to try to get in that way, but that door is mostly closed, so I wasn't sure what I was to do. My chest felt as though it was going to burst with fear, but then I realized the people had removed her from the room and I could get in quite safely. Phew, I was so relieved, because she is very frightening and tries to bite my throat—which is really not very friendly.

I was a bit worried after a few days because she was allowed back into the place where they make the food, and so I lingered outside waiting for them to move her. They didn't, but they encouraged me to come in by offering me some treats, which I wasn't going to refuse! So I came inside and, actually, I realized she couldn't get to me anyway because they were holding onto her. I had a happy shake and then triumphantly went through to the comfy room.

The people have somehow managed to stop her from chasing me, but I now think it can be quite good fun when she does. I do sometimes worry that the little dog doesn't really know the true meaning of the word 'play', though, and she thinks that playing means she can grab me with her teeth. At times she's a little bit gentler with me, and those are the times when I put my front legs down on the floor and my bottom in the air, and wait in front of her until she chases me. If she does start flashing those teeth at me, I've now realized I can get away from her. That's because I have long legs and I'm much faster than she is. I don't think it would be quite such fun if she actually caught me.

Mum (the woman of the house) seems to be sad. She still calls me Mumsboy, which makes me happy, but when we're all sitting around and having treats while the noisy box is on in the corner, she seems to be a little sad. I always try to make sure it's me who sits next to her. Then I put my face behind her while she strokes my back, and that's when I feel safe.

Tuesday August 5th

Not Such a Quiet Life

Peggy

A greyhound's retirement is meant to be just that—an opportunity to forget what has gone on before and just exist in a nice, peaceful life in a nice, calm home. Well, don't you just know that the little dog who lived with the old lady suddenly moved in with us? I'm not quite sure whose decision this was, but I was not happy about it, I can tell you! That nice, quiet retirement I am talking about is suddenly no longer possible. At first I wondered when she was going to leave again, but time has passed and she is still with us.

When she first came to live here I sensed there was something wrong with her. She seemed to be quite withdrawn and upset about something. She wasn't the only one—if I'm perfectly honest—the people here, too, they seemed to be miserable about something.

Well, what is a girl to do when that happens? I did all I could and went and put my head on their laps. There was only so much I could do though, because when everyone's upset, whose lap do you go and put your head on? Who do you try to console? In the end, I just decided I would have to share my affection around them all, and just picked whomever I thought was the saddest at that time. Sometimes the little dog didn't like me doing it, especially if she was already sitting next to someone, but I did what I could without her leaping at my face.

The little dog's old lady didn't seem to be around anymore, and when the little dog arrived, Ralph's person put her bed up in our bedroom. She also placed something in her bed that smelled of the old lady. I just couldn't believe it, the little dog had moved into our bedroom! What was that all about? Her bed was put beside Ralph's and when bed time came we got our treats as usual. I figured there might be an opportunity for me to steal some of the treats from the little dog like I sometimes do from Ralph. When I tried, she glared at me with those big, boggle eyes and put her head right over the treats so I couldn't get at them. She then pulled back her lips to reveal those tiny teeth.

When she initially arrived she did, indeed, sleep in her own bed. Not any more though! Oh no! She now sleeps on the bed where the humans sleep. Straight up on to the bed she goes and curls herself up right there between them. The cheek of her! At first they used to tell her to go back to her bed, but they no longer do that. As soon as she's had her bedtime treats, up onto the bed she goes. Personally I've never been so bothered about sleeping on the human bed as it gets a little warm, but you can tell Ralph is a bit fed up that she is allowed. He still goes up there occasionally, but not usually until the morning, and then only if the sun is shining through the window. He loves the sunshine.

Ah, yes, the sunshine. As with the human bed being a little warm for me, I also tend to avoid the sun. Not Ralph, though. He'll lie with the sun streaming through the windows until he's breathing really hard and his tongue is hanging out of his mouth. He'll do the same when the back doors are open and he lies out on the grass panting away to himself in the bright sunshine. Madness! Utter madness!

I've noticed that when he goes out there on really hot days his person puts some white stuff on his face and ears. I don't know whether that makes him pant or what, but it does seem to be quite strange behaviour. I only go out there to do my necessaries—you wouldn't catch me lying out there in that heat.

The little dog, though, she loves the sunshine as well and sometimes the two of them compete for sunny spots, which can be quite amusing to watch. Yes, it is quite funny watching as they try and nudge each other out of the way into the shade.

The sofa, though, I guess that's where we all compete for space. Luckily there's one each, but this often means the humans have to go and sit on floppy cushions on the floor. They don't seem to mind. When visitors come over we have to relent and give up our spaces, and before they arrive for some reason the man and woman of the house change the sofa coverings. I don't know why. After all, they smell quite nicely of us. Anyway, when those visitors come, Ralph is extremely cheeky as he goes up and stares at the people until they move up to make space for him. I think they let him because he's Ralph, and because they seem to always feel sorry for him. They somehow appear to feel privileged that he wants to sit next to them. I suppose that because he's generally so wary of people, they just give into him, thinking they've suddenly become some sort of dog whisperer, whatever one of those is. And the little dog, well, she just forces herself in between whichever visitors happen to be sitting there. I don't see any dog whisperers offering to take *her* on. Only I am polite enough to understand that visitors have priority in that situation—and I certainly don't need any dog whisperers.

Monday August 18th

Back to work

Clare

I should feel refreshed and I'm absolutely worn out. Work began again today, and here we are in a new term with new students starting just next week.

When the holiday should have refreshed me, I haven't managed to rest, and feel I've hardly slept. I've finished writing *A Soldier Like Jack*, but at what cost? And for what purpose? I am utterly exhausted. Before Mum died I included her at every stage and she seemed to be proud of what I was trying to do. More importantly, she seemed to appreciate that her grandparents' story was finally going to be told. I am so glad she got to read a draft of it, but incredibly saddened that she wasn't able to see it in its final form.

I still feel I have to fill every minute of every day. Even when I appear to be resting, my mind is in overdrive and I am somewhere else. I am planning what I can do, what I can achieve, and how I can try to make a difference to this world. I constantly think about the world's environmental problems and how I can help in some way to raise awareness. In my less frantic times I attempt to keep myself occupied with walking the dogs, cooking, writing, even a household chore—anything that stops me from thinking about what has happened.

Lucy is a constant reminder of Mum, but I try to think of her now as being our dog, and not a little dog I have inherited. I know she misses Mum, and I think that sometimes I sound like Mum. I can hear it myself—especially when I call out Lucy's name in a certain way, elongating the syllables just like Mum used to. When I quite by accident do that, Lucy looks at me and tilts her head as though she's trying to figure something out. I then try to speak in my own voice, but it's hard—it can be difficult to fight your genetic and cultural legacy, and I guess Lucy and I just have to get used to the fact that I will from time to time sound just like Mum did.

The dogs were in on their own for a little while today. We're trying to get them used to sometimes having a few hours when there are no humans in the house. We've tried to do this at every opportunity during the summer holiday, but Anthony will be leaving to go back to university in a few weeks and we need to make it so that all three dogs are quite happy with a little non-human time. The dogs are actually getting along really well, and as time is passing I feel much more confident that they are going to be okay.

Peggy and Lucy seem to have agreed on some sort of truce, and will now sometimes be seen lying together at peace on the sofa or on a dog bed. I'd expected it to take longer than this and that we'd always be worried about them, but it's been okay. I say that with only the slightest bit of trepidation, because I guess you can never know for sure how a dog will react to another in the long term, or under different circumstances. I have to give most of the credit to the success of their apparent bonding to Peggy's ability to not react when Lucy is terrorizing her and Ralph. Her great patience and their being like this is helping me because it is one less thing to be worried about.

Much of Mum's copious amount of paperwork is now sorted out, but I have no idea what to do with her ashes. Since picking them up from the undertaker, the urn has been positioned on the sideboard next to the television, alongside a vase I constantly replenish with a succession of seasonal flowers. I keep looking at that urn and wondering what on Earth I am going to do with it.

When I got the urn home I morbidly wondered whether Lucy would be interested in it, but she's not. She seems to be quite indifferent about its presence—in fact, none of the dogs have shown any interest in it. This is quite odd, because normally any new object in the house has to undergo detailed canine scrutiny.

And so, the urn sits there while I think, and while I wait for my men folk to help me decide what we are going to do with its contents. So far they haven't been very forthcoming with ideas, constantly saying they'll leave it up to me.

In the meantime, I have work to consider and an impending new cohort of students. I'm glad, as too much time to think is not a good thing for me. I hope this new term is going to provide some welcome distractions.

Friday August 22nd

Home alone

Lucy

Ralph's person is no longer here all the time but goes away for short times and then comes back again. Sometimes the tall one isn't here either, so Ralph, Peggy and I are occasionally left on our own.

When they are all out, those are the times when the three of us can run rampage around the house. Well, Ralph and I do anyway. Ralph seems to have an obsession with collecting his person's things and will go around the place collecting her stuff. He pulls things from hooks and takes them from the backs of chairs. He leaves everything he's collected lying in a big pile in the middle of the hallway for her to find when she gets back. When she comes home, she picks them up and goes around the house putting them all back where Ralph found them. This is only for Ralph, the next time she goes out, to go around the house and remove them all again.

He's strange that Ralph-dog. He has a much-loved chair that he lies on when the people are out or when they are making food. He is actually a bit too large for the chair, but he somehow manages to squash himself in it. I must say that I am actually quite partial to that seat myself. I often try to head for it before Ralph can get there, only most times and because of his long legs, Ralph gets there before I do. If he does and I want the seat, I stand next to him and make an angry rumble in my throat, but he just rests his head on the back of the chair and lies there looking out of the window. I fear he is taking more lessons from Peggy. As for Peggy, though, when the people are out she just disappears up the stairs and goes and lies on the landing where it is cool. She is absolutely no fun!

Before the people leave us on our own there is always the same routine: out for a pee, and then back into the house for a treat before they leave. Ralph is odd because he likes the boring treats that Peggy and I don't like, so he clears up those ones while pointy-face and I try to eat the tasty ones as quickly as we can.

Peggy has a long mouth with big teeth, so I sometimes have to surrender and let her have the last tasty morsel. Once we get to that stage and the people have gone and there's no hope of any more treats, satisfied, she goes and lies up the stairs. Meanwhile, Ralph and I clear up the remnants of the boring biscuits. Mostly Ralph, though, because if anyone thinks I am going to consume sub-standard treats, they have another thing coming!

Sunday August 30th

Dogs, Dogs . . . and More Dogs

Clare

Anthony is returning to university and the dogs will miss him—especially Peggy. When we haven't been watching or noticing, he and Peggy have forged a strong bond. When he works, she lies by his side; when he rests, she will be there resting beside him, hanging onto his every word. When he joins us on our walks, he's most likely to be the human on the other end of her lead. As the next stage after his PhD will most likely be working away from our home town, we realize the separation except for visits is most likely to be a permanent one. So, while still dealing with our own bereavement, Peggy is about to be suffering a loss of her own, albeit a sporadic one.

When Anthony is home from university, he is far more conscientious than me or Bob at regular playtime in the garden with the dogs. We do the majority of the walks, he throws balls for them. Anthony's adoring Peggy isn't so interested in play. She gets fed up after a few throws of the ball, and I'm sure she thinks to herself, 'Why should a greyhound run if she doesn't HAVE to?' Ralph and Lucy, however, love to play. Lucy is very mouthy as she enthusiastically charges around the garden, and sometimes quite worryingly, jumps up at Ralph and tries to nip at his throat. Meanwhile, Ralph plays with her much more nicely, pouncing around flinging his big paws about in such a way that you sometimes imagine he might just flatten her! But he is so delicate and gentle—he would never hurt her.

In the right environment and with suitable littermates dogs, like wolves, learn to inhibit aggression at an early age. When they play too rough they are immediately apprehended by their brothers and sisters. A squeal or a bite back usually does the trick. It's just not in an animal's interests to expend too much energy on fighting unless they have to—it simply isn't an evolutionarily viable strategy. I don't, however, think Lucy ever learned how to inhibit aggression. She enters a sort of turbo-charged way of behaving when she feels as though she's in control and has to sort out one of the other dogs. She does this far more with Ralph than with Peggy—Peggy would simply not let her get away with it. While Ralph will absolutely back off, Peggy will sometimes snarl, but luckily she has that innate bite inhibition and never allows it to escalate. It's definitely Peggy who will eventually back off if there is a confrontation—never Lucy!

On our regular walks Lucy has now encountered most of the local dogs, and there seems to be no rhyme or reason dictating which dogs she will like, and which of them she will immediately raise her lips to:

Next door there are two dogs: Rosa the chocolate Labrador and Tessa a small mixed breed. The fence separating the two gardens, and therefore the two sets of dogs from one another, provides some sense of security for them, and therefore the opportunity for them all to defend their own territories. We've blocked up the bottom half of each vertical gap in the fence so they can't constantly antagonize each other through it.

With that terrier determination, it wasn't long before Lucy managed to find another way. She's discovered that if she digs down a little and makes a hole in the dirt between the plants, she can create a small gap and can snuffle through the fence and entice Tessa to come and bark at her. Then, once the other dog has responded, Lucy has a good old growl, raises her hackles and generally winds everyone up. At this point, the competing 'packs' of dogs will race up and down the garden having a good old woof at one another.

Ralph's strategy to attract next door's dogs' attention is quite different in that he, being much taller, realized very quickly that if he sits at the point where our garden has an incline, he can see through the gaps between the wood in the unblocked top half of the fence. He sometimes sits there for hours when the weather is nice, waiting to see whether he can spot Rosa out in the garden. This is just so he can instigate a session of barking and running up and down the length of the fence. For Rosa is their great prize; it is her reaction they're all after! Being a Labrador, her bark is louder and she gives them more to bark back at. Even lazy Peggy joins in when she knows Rosa is outside.

Like so many dogs, Ralph adores sitting outside in the sunshine! This is to the extent that he has to wear sunscreen on his prominent white parts, particularly the top of his muzzle and his (almost) bald chest. I've seen many dogs and cats with skin cancer, so it's better to be safe and provide him with some protection. I don't know why he has a bald chest. There's no sign of any skin infection or inflammation there, and the rest of him is fine—he just has very little fur on the area around his sternum. In the summer he has fine, downy hair there, but in the winter he even loses that and becomes pretty well bald in that region. I suspect the warmth of the central heating plays a huge part in his body getting mixed up with the time of year! So Ralph waits in the garden, sunscreen slathered on his belly and face, and watches out for next door's dogs to communicate with.

Peggy will either take or leave other dogs, and is generally rather aloof and nonchalant whenever she encounters them. She loves other greyhounds, however, and seems to be able to spot them from a long way off; perhaps it's that shared history they sense, and the distinct shape they have which makes for easy 'non-verbal' communication.

The only type of dog Peggy has never particularly shown a liking for is the dreaded black Labrador. Yellow and chocolate ones are fine, but not black ones. When she first came to live with us she had a couple of altercations with black Labradors, and I suppose those confrontations have stuck in her memory. She doesn't appreciate dogs jumping up and leaping at her face and snarled at two of them who did this to her. I imagine she's never quite forgotten those occasions and now, in her humble greyhound opinion, it appears that all black Labradors have been tarred with the same brush.

This meant that when we moved into this house, local resident black Labradors Louis and Murphy were onto a losing thing when they first encountered Peggy. She's not aggressive towards them; she simply doesn't even look in their direction. When Ralph sees either of them he prances around in great enthusiasm. In the early days Louis used to do the same thing back to Ralph, but big, strong Louis seems to have matured, unlike Ralph, who continues to dance around in front of most dogs he meets. And Lucy? Well Lucy doesn't really like Labradors. Perhaps I should rephrase that: Lucy doesn't like most dogs . . .

There are some dogs Lucy does tolerate, and Murphy is one of them. Murphy is a calm and gentle old chap. He is getting on in years and, probably very wisely, doesn't really make eye contact with Lucy. Another dog she tolerates is old Laddie the Border collie. Again, he is quite old, and for the most part he doesn't make eye contact with any of our dogs.

Perhaps these two old boys have learned, like Peggy, that it's sometimes easier to get on in life if you just don't bother communicating with the smaller canine troublemakers, which is probably quite a sound survival strategy. By making eye contact you are giving an indication of a willingness to partake in a canine to canine 'conversation', which with little dogs could be either a pleasurable one, or one that you would rather not have.

Ralph tries to 'speak' to both Murphy and Laddie, but neither of them has ever been particularly interested in what he has to offer! While we're talking to their respective humans, Murphy will let out a big sigh and lie down, whereas Laddie will go on ahead and patiently wait for the human conversation to end. They are extremely wise old dogs—and there is something very special about an old dog!

I sometimes think that underneath all the bravado Lucy is actually a little wary of other dogs, particularly if they are larger than her. She seems to express an element of fear, caution or nervousness as being something akin to the need to let them know who is boss.

There are a lot of small dogs around here for her to boss around, and without exception, Lucy likes to express her loathing for them:

Alfie and Dexter are cousins to one another—sort of cousins anyway. They belong to two sisters who live a few doors from one another. They're both extremely small breeds—Alfie is a Yorkshire terrier and Dexter is a tiny, pale tan Chihuahua. The two of them get along with one another since they have grown up together, however neither of them is particularly fond of other dogs! What they're both united in, however, is their love for Ralph. Dexter is a similar shade of tan to Ralph, and when the two of them stand side by side it looks as though Ralph is standing next to a mini version of himself!

With Alfie, the fact that his name rhymes with Ralphie has probably encouraged Ralph and Alfie's enthusiasm for one another, and whenever we see him out and about walking with his family, we can't help ourselves excitedly declaring, 'Looooook, Ralphiiiieeee, it's Alfiiiieeee!' With Alfie's people doing the same to Alfie, the two dogs are always extremely happy to see one another. This tiny Yorkshire terrier and our huge, big-footed Ralph dance around one another. As she usually does, Peggy spends the whole time gazing off into the distance, desperate for Ralph's antics to be over. Lucy? Well, just like with Labradors, Lucy doesn't like Yorkshire terriers, doesn't like Chihuahuas and will, not surprisingly, growl at both of them.

Dexter the Chihuahua is the smallest dog I've seen for a very long time. He's slender and has a certain look of fragility about him. He and Ralph are always excited to meet up with one another, and Ralph allows Dexter to jump up towards his face and touch his cheeks or muzzle with his tiny paws. Ralph could easily flatten little Dexter with one swipe of one of his large feet, but he seems to adore little dogs—especially Dexter and Alfie. Not so big dogs! Just a few days ago he came across a massive Bernese mountain dog and veered a large semi-circle around him. He couldn't have made it more obvious that he was not going to be partaking in any canine communication with this bear-like creature.

Lucy's introduction to the dogs on our regular local routes has been interesting, especially as she was sort of the new kid on the block for a while and had to fit in with them all. Unfortunately, Lucy's idea of fitting in is baring her teeth and growling. Her reaction to them is something we have to manage. She is improving as time goes by, but she does have one particular least-favourite dog.

This dog is a miniature schnauzer. There are two miniature schnauzers living nearby, but it is only one of them that she really doesn't like. I don't know whether it is the cut of his hair which creates that extremely defined square schnauzer face, or whether they have some kind of personality clash that is not evident to us humans. When she sees him she growls, she grumbles, bares her teeth and yanks at the lead to try and reach him. Meanwhile, the schnauzer tries desperately not to make eye contact and veers his owner in a different direction away from the tyrant that is Lucy. Perhaps we have to accept that she can sometimes demonstrate these terrier 'in for the kill' characteristics.

As with Ralph and Peggy, we don't know what Lucy encountered in her pre-rescue life, and while she does exhibit these dog to dog aggressive responses, she's not uncontrollable. Optimistically, I've been training her by rewarding her to instead focus her attention on me or whoever else is walking her. This does seem to help, but you can often see that terrier instinct taking over, and she makes sure she has her say before she eventually complies and focuses her attention where it is meant to be. You can see the inner turmoil in her face and body as she almost bursts with frustration at not being allowed to be nasty.

There are a couple of dogs Lucy doesn't respond to in an especially negative way. I won't say she never does, or will never do so in the future, as that would be an incredible leap of faith due to Lucy's element of unpredictability. There are two Charlies living nearby, and they are both really such gentle creatures. One is a Blenheim Cavalier King Charles spaniel; the other a sensitive little black and tan crossbreed. Both these dogs are extremely sweet natured, and perhaps Lucy senses this and their vulnerability and, not wanting to be a bully, leaves them alone so she won't upset them. Or perhaps because she won't get a reaction she just doesn't think they're worth the effort . . . I like to think that it's the former, but I admit to having my doubts about this.

Wednesday September 10th

Cat Alley

Clare

It is not only dogs we encounter on our three walks a day. The area in which we live is still being built, and with more people coming into the area there are naturally more cats moving in. We therefore come across cats, many cats in fact. I think with this area being quite far away from any major roads, it has become a haven for cat lovers. We love cats too and with previous dogs we always had cats living with us, but as they died off we didn't replace them—mostly because we had moved by that time to a busy road, but also because we had never been very lucky with the cats we had in our lives and decided we were jinxed. More recently, it has been because we know that our normally gentle Peggy would absolutely never allow a cat to come anywhere near the house.

Ralph, though, expressed really early on that he would love us to have a cat. There used to be a local Birman, with those typical to the breed white 'boxing gloves' on the end of each of his four paws. Ralph loved him, and whenever the cat came up to us in the street he used to roll over on his back and allow Ralph to nuzzle his tummy. While Ralph did this, Peggy expressed her gross distaste by growling and trying to pull Bob towards the cat. I hate to say that I don't think she wanted to partake in any tummy-snuffling!

Peggy's apparent loathing for cats is one reason why we never allow her to run off the lead. The other reason is her desperate noise phobia. Anything that sounds remotely like a firework (cars backfiring, crow scarers, thunder) will make her run, and as we all know, greyhounds can run! When she has a fright she tends to lose any sense of direction. Even if she's in the house or garden when it happens, she immediately becomes a quivering wreck and heads for cover; she won't eat, and won't respond if we try to distract her. We simply have to give her time to come around.

The Birman cat disappeared. I think he moved away, but there are still plenty of cats around to keep all three dogs entertained. Lucy used to be okay with cats, and I know this for sure from the walks I used to take her on when I sometimes walked her for Mum. She never responded in a negative way to cats that were walking past, on someone's doorstep, or sitting perched on a fence. Lucy one day came nose to nose with a pretty, grey cat that was taking itself for a stroll in the park. There was no negative reaction from Lucy whatsoever, to the extent that the two curious creatures sniffed each other for some time. Eventually the cat decided it was the end of the feline to canine conversation, flicked her pedigree Russian blue tail and wandered off with said tail in the air. Lucy's tolerance of cats is unfortunately not so any longer. You would hope that she would have learned some of the nice, delicate attitude that Ralph has towards cats, but I guess that being a terrier if she saw another dog respond in the way that Peggy does, well, I would imagine Peggy's way of behaving to dog's 'greatest enemy' would appear to be much more fun. Lucy being Lucy, that's surely a much more tempting way to behave!

So, while Ralph looks out for cats in the hope that one of them might just allow him to nuzzle their tummy, Lucy and Peggy look out for them so they can bark and snarl at them. The two of them have become an almost formidable force: canine partners in crime!

There's a local walkway we've nicknamed 'cat alley'. Cat alley is a place where cats go to linger, and seemingly to watch out for the likes of Lucy and Peggy; unfortunately poor old cat-loving Ralph gets tarred with the same brush. The cats hide underneath cars, on top of fence posts or walls, in bushes or the undergrowth, and some even blatantly sit on their own doorstep watching out for passing canines. Admittedly, some do run off or slink away and hide when they see our three riotous brutes coming along (well, two really). Some, though, hold their ground and if the dogs dare to look in their direction, the cats arch their backs, and up come their hackles.

Unfortunately for Ralph he often bears the brunt of the semi-hidden cats. This is because, being male, he spends a lot more time sniffing around the bushes and undergrowth—places where the cats tend to hide. He frequently gets a shock as some angry feline suddenly comes rushing out of the bushes and shrieks at him as it goes racing past. I'm sure the cat is equally-shocked when they sense the large dog investigating their hiding place.

We've learned from the dogs' antics, and lately if we see any obvious feline presence we divert our walk and go around the long way, often avoiding cat alley all together. It's so much easier for dogs, cats or humans to avoid any preventable canine versus feline strife.

Wednesday September 17th

On Lucy and Peggy

Ralph

The creatures with the pointed ears seem to be outnumbering us dogs around here. Some of them are fun, like the one who rolls over on his back to let me snuffle his tummy, although I haven't seen him for a while. There are some frightening ones, too, though! They are the ones who linger in the bushes waiting to attack me as I walk past. They sit there, silently waiting for me to come along and have an innocent sniff at the leaves, and then they come darting out of the bush, giving me quite a shock!

There's one place we go where there are lots of them, and I mean LOTS! When we walk along there I just don't know where to look. Sometimes, if I'm feeling especially brave, I wag my tail at them and let out a playful woof. If some of the nastier ones are around, though, I just pretend I haven't seen them, and certainly don't make eye contact with them. Even so, they just sit there and stare at me with their paws crossed—some of them even lazily wash their paws while they're staring, which is really quite clever when you think about it.

The little dog with the teeth is still here. I think she must be living with us now, which is nice and all that, but she doesn't seem to have lost that competitive streak. She always has to be the first to the chair, the first to the food, and the first to go to the people when they say my most-loved word, which is 'Walkies!' Sometimes the people try to disguise that word by saying something which sounds like 'Double U,' but they're not fooling me, I know that means the same thing.

Anyway, back to the little dog, in my opinion, I think she's actually an attention-seeker! She still chases me out of the house when I come back from my pre-dinner evening pee in the garden. I've got used to her doing it now and just let her—I know she can't catch me. Not every time anyway. She is so little and her legs are very short, but sometimes she jumps up and tries to grab me around the throat, which really isn't very friendly.

And then with our food, mine and Peggy's, she tries to reach the bowls, but because they are high off the ground, she can only just get her face in Peggy's bowl, but not mine, because mine is the highest bowl. That's because I am the tallest dog in the house—I am even taller than Peggy. The little dog does try to reach my bowl, oh, how she tries, but she just can't. The only way she manages to get the food is if she knocks the bowl holder over. She has done this a few times. I don't think that pleases Mum and the man, though, because they have to clear up all the food from the floor!

I've been introducing the little dog to all the dogs who live near to us, although I do wish she would behave herself! It is just a bit annoying when I'm trying to say hello to one of them and she's there with her teeth showing. It's really not pleasant of her to do that and have that nasty sound rumbling from her throat. I don't know what is wrong with her, because the dogs around here are all really nice and friendly.

The dogs I like the most are two tiny ones—Alfiiiieeee and Dexter. I especially like Alfiiiieeee because his name sounds a bit like mine, and we both jump around and get excited whenever we meet. Peggy doesn't really communicate with any of the other dogs and just stares off into the distance wanting to go home. I think she's just lazy because she always wants the walks to be as short as possible. She would far rather be at home lying on the soft seats and eating treats!

Wednesday October 8th

On Other Creatures

Peggy

As time's gone by the little dog has become somewhat of an appendage. She won't leave me alone. She seems to think I am her long-lost mother and keeps on reaching up and licking my mouth. Other times you'd think she was *my* mother as she insists on washing my privates. I can't quite make her out. She is so very changeable—one minute she is all sweet and affectionate, and the next she is quite horrible and trying to leap at mine or Ralph's throat. Every now and then I raise my lips and show her my big, sharp teeth, and do you know what she does? She stands right in front of me and shows me those tiny little teeth in her mouth. Not being a bully, that's when I back off. I figure you'll never win with someone like that, so it's better to just avoid them when they're in that sort of mood.

Ralph, though, he can be a bit silly sometimes and seems to think she's playing, so he prances about in front of her. Quite dangerously so, in my opinion. Sometimes she does leap at him, but he seems to think it's all a big game, so he carries on jumping around her and going down on his front paws and offering little woofs; a very dangerous strategy, I think! The little dog is actually very grumpy with all the other animals around these parts, especially the dogs. The cats as well, but they perhaps deserve her grumpiness. That's one thing on which we do agree!

I have to admit that I'm not that keen on cats. I've experienced far too many of them trying to swipe me across the face. Honestly, they have. They lurk in the bushes and wait for you to come along. Then, wham, up come their hackles (and mine), and we have a stand-off. There was one in the back garden one day and I chased it. I'm very fast, but then at the last second up it went. It scaled the fence and I saw it jump down on the other side. I didn't see it in the garden again! Ralph saw it, too, but he seems to like those nasty, evil creatures and followed me as I chased it, but he wasn't chasing it for the same reason I was. The idiotic dog wanted to play with it. Does he not know that this is really not acceptable canine behaviour?

It was actually yours truly who taught the little one; she now knows the mantra: *'Cats are NOT our friends!'* Perhaps Ralph will learn one day. I doubt it, though, he's gone so far down the road of being a cat enthusiast that there's little hope for him. There are times when he even washes himself like a cat does—perhaps he actually thinks he is a cat? Now that IS a disturbing thought.

Now, rabbits? There are a lot of those long-eared creatures around these parts. I used to think it would be entertaining to chase them—just like I used to have to chase that furry thing back in my old racing days. The humans here, though, they tricked me and gave me treats whenever I didn't pay any attention to the rabbits. So I don't really bother any more. I'll do pretty much anything for a treat. Whichever human designed this way of dog training, well, I think they should be knighted. That person is a genius. Sometimes there are no food treats, however, and I just get told I'm a 'good girl', but I think treats should be given anyway if you do something that's good, otherwise it's a bit deceptive of these humans!

I love it when visitors come over. When this happens I offer them my toy when they come through the door. I used to try and jump up and say a proper hello to them, but then I was taught I had to carry a toy instead. For being good I get a treat. I almost always get one for doing this, and I don't know why some 'good girl' events are worth more treats than others. Then when the humans sit down to eat we usually get a long-lasting treat. I think this is so I don't go and put my head on the table while they're eating.

I've learnt, though, that if I finish my long-lasting treat quickly, by going and seeing how the people are getting along with their food, I get another long-lasting treat to eat while everyone else finishes eating. This includes Ralph and the little dog—they're so slow at eating treats—just because it says it's long-lasting doesn't mean you have to stretch it out. Not at all, eat it as fast as possible and then you get more, that's my motto!

One thing I don't appreciate is when I hear a loud bang. I'm rarely ever sure where the loud bang is coming from. Sometimes the loud noise sounds as though it's coming from the sky, sometimes from those vehicle things, and sometimes from bright lights that zoom into the air. There are times when the sound happens time and time again and I can't get away from it. There we might be, going for a nice gentle walk and then, boom! When that happens I feel the most awful pain shoot across my chest and my head hurts. I get into a panic and I pull on the lead; I keep on pulling until we get home. When we get home, I go and find a dark corner and sit shaking and shaking. Nothing will console me: not food, not treats, not the offer of going on the sofa for a cuddle.

Nothing.

I just have to wait until I'm sure that the sound is not going to happen again and then, eventually, I'll tentatively accept a treat. And the tastier the treat is the better.

The tall one has gone missing again. I've become very attached to him because he rubs my ears and lets me go and lie on his bed when he's up there watching one of those boxes with the pictures on them. He went away before and then came back again, so I hope he does this soon. I miss him. Ralph's person opens his room up for me so I can go in there and have a lie down, but it's not the same when he isn't in there with me.

Saturday November 8th

Those Pesky Fireworks and a New 'New Kid on the Block'

Clare

Shortly after we moved here Ralph struck up a friendship with Sandy, a man who lives nearby. This was incredibly unusual because Ralph doesn't really socialize with people, but even more so, it was strange because Ralph doesn't really like men. In a desperate attempt to make friends with Ralph, Sandy would crouch down to get close to him. He very quickly learned not to reach out to touch Ralph, and to avoid looking directly into his eyes.

Eventually, in the same way that Ralph dances around when he sees another dog, he also began to do it whenever he saw Sandy. At last Ralph was making some headway in dealing with his fear of people, and especially men. Since then, he has indeed become much braver with everyone when we're out on our walks, but not to the extent that he would allow them to touch him on his head. I doubt that will ever change; I think we shall always have to make sure everyone knows to give him some space.

It would have been easier to have got Ralph used to meeting people had he been food orientated, and therefore willing to accept treats from strangers, but his overbearing nervousness has always been a distraction for him. Even with the confidence he has gained, his reluctance to be around new people will always be a barrier for him.

For a long time Sandy had wanted to have a dog of his own and, finally, he and his wife brought a little Lhasa apso puppy home to live with them. Ralph was really NOT amused when he first encountered this ball of black and white fluff. As a young puppy, Chester was offered down to Ralph to allow them to sniff one another. At this, Ralph looked the other way, clearly demonstrating a Peggy-like display of a lack of interest. Meanwhile, Peggy was her usual aloof self—and Lucy, well, true to form she gave Chester a deep growl and flashed her teeth. No dog is immune from Lucy's domineering personality—not even a tiny puppy. I do wonder with Lucy, however, how much of this is still related to her being the new dog in the area, and that she is trying to establish herself in this new life she's been forced into.

As Chester has grown over the last few weeks, Ralph has found much greater appeal in the playful individual he has become, seeming to forgive Chester's people for 'replacing him' with this tiny ball of fluff. Meanwhile, Lucy continues to treat the said fluff-ball with a great deal of disdain, and Peggy's aloofness towards him hasn't faltered.

Chester is one of those brave little dogs—one who isn't

overwhelmed by much; he's a dog who confronts everything in his path with the same degree of enthusiasm and confidence. He's having a good upbringing with a family who love him very much, so all his learning and memories are wrapped up in them and the way his life is with them.

Conversely, like many rescue dogs, our three have all come to us with baggage of varying degrees. This even applies to Peggy, but her problems originate from her being noise phobic—something she shares with many dogs. In the lead-up to Guy Fawkes, we found ourselves having to prepare ourselves for our annual battle of bonfire night.

Remember, remember the 5th November.

Oh, how we can never miss 5th November. In our town the night time becomes something akin to a warzone with bright lights, loud bangs, and the strong stench of smoke lingering in the air. The problem would be manageable if the fireworks were restricted to just one night of the year—even two, Guy Fawkes and then New Year, but it goes on for weeks. We anticipate them to go on over the coming few weekends, but who knows, perhaps it will rain and no one will bother.

If it were just a couple of nights, we could close all the curtains, put the radio on in every room, and the television on nice and loudly in the sitting room. To do this every night for a whole month is just impractical, though, and to be expected to tranquillize your dog for the whole period would be completely unreasonable. Instead, we have to do what we can to protect Peggy from the sounds, and just make sure we don't go out for walks at high risk times. Even the pre-bedtime walk sometimes brings a stray firework sound in the distance, and that's when Peggy bolts. Just one firework can make her miserable, terrified, shaking, and off her food for hours.

Peggy's obviously not alone in her phobia, and all over the world people who share their lives with animals have to battle with the consequences of fireworks; the celebration of some has become the nightmare of many.

We didn't know what to expect from Lucy with Guy Fawkes. I had a vague recollection from Mum that Lucy had not been bothered at all with the noise. And she isn't—to the extent that she's quite happy going into the garden to the toilet when all around us the sky is exploding with lights and crashing bangs. She seems positively fascinated with what's going on up there in the vivid, glowing, deafening sky.

Ralph is very reactive with this one—if he sees Peggy quivering he'll go over and lie next to her, and also start quivering; if he hears fireworks and he happens to be outside and doesn't see her reaction, he's absolutely fine. Lately, unfortunately, he has seemed to be leaning more towards the Peggy way of responding to fireworks, rather than picking up on the positive vibes from Lucy.

With this annual event in our canine calendar hopefully pretty much over and done with, we can now begin to prepare for Christmas—and Anthony will be home to catch up with his beloved Peggy.

With plenty of love she has coped with Anthony being away again. Recently, however, Bob and I brought home some boxes that Anthony wanted us to store. A few days after we had put them in his bedroom, I popped in there to look for a DVD he wanted us to post to him. Peggy followed me and spent a long time investigating the boxes we had brought back. There had been no food in them (which would normally have been her main attraction), but she investigated them for a long time. I guess that, despite all our efforts, she misses him a lot—even now a few months since he left.

Sunday December 27th

That First Christmas

Clare

Our first Christmas without Mum was never going to be easy. In the time leading up to the festive season, I wished I'd had the guts to say to everyone we should just forget about it for this year. I wished I could just slip inside a comfy cocoon for a few weeks and emerge from it in the New Year; refreshed, healed, and ready to move on. Life, somehow, gets in the way of what you want to do and, for fear of upsetting everyone else, you just get on with what is expected—however much hurt is going on inside.

All those memories of Christmases of the past that come to the fore during each festive season have seemed this year to somehow be much more vivid. The memory that has been most clear is of the Christmas we shared last year. Mum was here, and I can clearly remember thinking there would be many more Christmases to share with her: Ten? Fifteen? Even twenty or more?

Had we known that last year's Christmas was going to be the last one we would spend together, would we have made more effort? Would she have forced herself to have stayed awake longer on Christmas Day if she had known that those were the last Christmassy minutes we would ever share? Is it but a blessing that we don't ever know for sure which will be our last precious moments with our loved ones?

Last year Lucy had been but a visitor in our midst. She had been the little dog who had protected Mum from all the ills of the world, even those things she didn't need to protect her from. That was Lucy's will—her might, her mission.

Mum would have loved it here this Christmas. We were all at our house, and the three dogs allowed us to not dwell too much on Christmases of the past. Once I had realized I had no option but to go through with all the preparations, all the motions, it was a fun Christmas—we were determined to make it so. But amid all that determination, with all my resolve, inside me there was a sick feeling; a knot in my gut that kept on reminding me that something was missing.

Her.

My mum, our mum, Anthony's grandmother, Lucy's devoted companion.

She was missing.

She was missing from the preparations for lunch; the nut roasts; the veggie stuffing; the awful bread sauce I made and forced everyone to at least try; the vegan chocolate log that Anthony made; the coffee one I made; the exchange of presents; and seeing the dogs open up their gifts of new toys and chews. Chews that would keep them occupied while we all had a peaceful dinner. That was the general idea anyway.

Having Lucy here and knowing that Mum would have approved of how she is and how we are caring for her, that helps. It gives me a sense of comfort that attached to this small dog there is a piece of Mum. Mum lives on in us and also in this creature she cared so much about. This little dog gives me an extra sense of purpose; a purpose that is directly connected to her.

The familiar scents of Christmas are all here. They're oozing into our pores and making us happy, and I now realize that perhaps my idea of cancelling Christmas would not have been such a good one. Just getting on with it has been the best thing for us to do. I imagine it is also what Mum would have wanted.

Raising a glass to Mum's memory at dinner on Christmas Day, I nearly faltered, nearly lost my sense of my place in time and broke down, but I managed to hold it together to avoid upsetting us all. Perhaps there's something in that? Perhaps we appear to cope with loss for everyone else's sake, and being able to sometimes suppress how you really feel is part of the road to recovery? Perhaps it's some internal ceremony we perform as we squash our feelings into the compressed pit of our selves.

Mum's photographs provide a reminder of how she

looked, but I find I can't linger and look at them for long. Beyond that, I've realized I can't remember her voice. I still think Lucy sometimes hears her in my own voice. Sometimes when I say something I sense her doing a double-take. Her head cocks to one side and she looks puzzled. Does she still get confused and remember? I don't know. I really don't.

I feel I haven't properly grieved. I feel as though inside me there's a volcano simmering, waiting to erupt. But it's not yet time for the explosion; for now I have things to do. I have to ease the pain for the others, and for Lucy. I have to be there to make sure their own volcanoes remain intact; to stop the lava from bubbling over; to smooth the ripples and keep life rumbling along.

A previous principal from the college in which I teach used to liken me to a carthorse. He said it to me a few times over the years, and I used to wonder what he meant. A group of students from about the same era likened me to an Irish setter. Only in recent years have I seen what they both meant. I think he was implying that I have the strength and will of a carthorse and that, conversely, the students possibly saw the light-hearted side of me. Perhaps they saw the side that's fun, scatter-brained—even unintentionally ditsy at times.

This last year I've seen the darker side of the carthorse and less of that fun-loving Irish setter. The darker side of the carthorse is that of the beast of burden—the horse that is weighed down by the loads of man; the Irish setter is what I long to be.

There was a picture on our childhood wall of some mountains, and the deeper the mountains reached into the depths of the image, the purpler they became. I think they were a picture of The Alps. It's likely Dad would have seen those mountains when he was in the army in the 1950s, and I wonder whether that's why we had the picture on the wall. Mum would never have seen them—and I know she didn't see the mountains of Scotland.

They both saw Mount Snowdon—does that compensate for not having ventured much farther away from home? The mountains of Wales are beautiful, and does one mountain range look pretty much the same as another? So does it really matter if you haven't seen all the world has to offer? Just so long as you're at peace with what you've done and what you've seen? As long as you're content with the life that you've carved for yourself?

The thing is, though, I don't know that she was actually happy with her lot; that she was happy with all she had done with her life. She encountered so much worry and grief, and if grief such as that goes unchecked it can consume someone.

When I look now at the photographs of her—pictures that show us together on so many Christmases, I think that for much of the time she was able to suppress the grief; store it in some deep cavern. But I think that as she got older and it was just her along with her succession of dogs, perhaps that was when she had more time to think; more time to have regrets. I think that was when her lifetime of grief and regret really did destroy her.

We didn't always see eye to eye and I think that's what makes losing her more difficult. Even though I spoke to her the day before she died, that conversation was unusually stilted. We'd put to the back of our minds all the problems of years ago and reached a plateau which allowed us to be mother and daughter. But still, as I put the phone down that day, I felt an emptiness I'd never felt before, and it's hard now to think whether I could have said something that would have changed the way things turned out.

Mum suffered horribly from the side-effects of tranquillizer withdrawal. She'd taken tranquillizers for eighteen years after Dad died, and withdrawal was enforced by the medical profession due to the long-term damage the benzodiazepines were causing people. While as a family we had been coping with the mental health problems that resulted from that, the real problems in mine and Mum's relationship initially had a lot to do with my moving thirty-five miles away. I had to do this to settle closer to work because the hour-long drive each way had been difficult. I think because of this I was never forgiven for taking her only grandchild away from her. We saw her every week, but I now think that in her situation it wasn't enough for her; that she needed more from me. And that's hard to come to terms with. I think I also expected more from her as my mother, and I didn't understand that her mental illness would sometimes not allow that to happen. I just feel that somehow for many years we didn't get that balance right.

While the problems began with our moving away, I think that was only the trigger for years of pent-up feelings and frustrations Mum needed to release about her own life, and we became the focus and bore the brunt of all her sadness and anger.

Over the years that spanned from 1993 to 2002, she seemed unable to accept my being with Bob and living in another town, and her resentment manifested itself in the most terrible rejection. I think all along she needed some psychiatric support, but any suggestions of this by me, Martin or her doctor were repeatedly met with a stone wall.

It was eventually Bob's donation of a kidney to me after I'd spent a year on dialysis which seemed to trigger her getting better. On the evening of the operation and in my hardly-lucid state, I phoned her. While I've no recollection of that phone call, Mum viewed the transplant itself as some kind of miracle—this man who had stolen me away from her had saved my life. That phone call triggered something in her that she referred to many times in the years to come. In the days and weeks that followed, she finally sought help for the demons that had been haunting her for so long. The psychiatrist prescribed a tiny little pill that made all the difference to her for the rest of her life. Whatever mental illness had prevented her from being happy during those years; that cloud had lifted.

I finally had my Mum back.

What was strange was how she seemed to block out those nine years of problems—just as though they had never happened. For the last twelve years of her life I had back the mum who had brought my brother and me up through such difficult circumstances. And that was the most wonderful thing in the world.

2015

Hogmanays Past and Present

Saturday January 3rd

Clare

When a new year arrives you resolve to do your best to lose weight, eat more healthily, do the things you promised yourself you would always do—including ticking things off your bucket list. But the days roll into weeks, and before you know it you're waving goodbye to the year in which you said you would do those things, and saying, 'Oh well, maybe we'll do those things this coming year?' Well, this year I have resolved to take Lucy to see the mountains of Scotland. A visit to the Alps shown in the painting I remember from the wall of my childhood home would mean pet passports and lots of travelling—and Lucy is not the best at travelling—but the Scottish mountains we can manage.

As we walk along the glaciated valleys and gaze up at the mountains, I shall think of Mum and Dad, and know they would have appreciated the beauty of the sky, and those distant purple mountain ranges will be ones that shall remind me of the picture they so carefully placed on their sitting room wall.

The dogs will enjoy a holiday too. They all like to investigate new places and sniff out the local dog population. Having three dogs does make it a little more difficult to find places to stay, but we have found a tiny, stone, whitewashed cottage which is situated at the foot of the hills on the far side of the Isle of Skye.

The dogs have been getting along fine through the holidays. Christmas was peaceful, and Lucy seems to no longer feel as though she has to defend anyone from Ralph and Peggy. It's as though she realizes we're all fairly capable of looking after ourselves. She does watch us, though, constantly keeping an eye on us—just to make sure!

Our last dog Oskar used to be food and toy possessive, which at times could be difficult to manage. Lucy is toy possessive, not so with food though, unless they are highly-coveted treats. With regular dog kibble, she seems to realize there is plenty to go around. I think Oskar had been affected early on by his lengthy period in rescue kennels and thought every meal was his last.

What Lucy doesn't realize, however, is that neither Ralph nor Peggy, and certainly not any of us, are the remotest bit interested in her toys. She likes the hard rubber toys that she can carry around in her mouth and flaunt at the other two. Peggy, however, loves soft toys because she can fulfill her maternal instincts and carry them around in her mouth as though they're puppies. Ralph is much more partial to toys that squeak.

Needless to say, Christmas has been extremely noisy—particularly as the dog toy manufacturers appear to have created an indestructible squeak!

Few dogs like the vets, and each year in winter the dogs are due for their annual check-up and vaccinations. I have to admit that this first visit with Lucy to our own vets instilled in me a tiny sense of dread.

At her previous practice Lucy committed a major felony and bit the vet. Neither Mum nor I had been with her at the time because she had been admitted to have her fractured canine tooth removed. She apparently struggled when they were trying to give her an anaesthetic, and that struggle culminated in the vet receiving a bite on his hand. When we went to collect her the bite was plain for all to see. Sensing the degree of throbbing from his swollen thumb, I reassured him that should she ever need to be an in-patient in the future, I would remain with her while she had the anaesthetic induced.

So, earlier today, there she was, going to try out her new veterinary surgery. And, very surprisingly for us, she was absolutely fine. Perhaps having Ralph and Peggy there gave her a little more confidence. I do sometimes think that her terrier ways are just bravado—and that really, deep down inside her, she's not that different to any other dog.

What probably doesn't help Lucy is that her vision is not

great—she even occasionally mistakes objects for being other animals. When we go for walks, for instance, she will sometimes raise her lips and put her hackles up at something inanimate like a pair of stone wellingtons that are adorning someone's front garden.

Ralph and Peggy have seemed over this first Christmas to have accepted that Lucy is going to be with us for the long haul. She is not going back to the old lady, because the old lady is no longer around. They can't know that for sure, but I do wonder whether they are curious about what happened to Mum. Whatever their understanding of this is, there does appear to be an acknowledgement that things have changed; that they all just have to get along and be happy in their group of three.

Saturday January 10th

Contemplations on Christmas and Stuff

Lucy

The vets!

I hate going to those places. They smell of fear, and there are always lots of animals queued up, all sitting quivering next to their people. All of them, every single one, is waiting to go and be tortured by someone with sharp tools that they stick in your skin, and cold, hard objects they push deep inside your ears.

Peggy and Ralph don't appear to like going there much either, so at least when we go, we're all in it together. We were there lately to see a woman who did all the torture things. I showed her my teeth to tell her to back off, but still she stabbed me with one of those very sharp objects. Right in the back of my neck!

The last wee while has been full of ups and downs, and up until recently in the main room we had one of those strange trees which has all the annoying flashing lights. I found it to be very confusing because it made me think a lot about the old woman. The last time there were all those smells around, she was there too. All the smells, the lights, the strangely-wrapped toys and chews, all of that was exactly the same as before; even the one who used to always come over and walk me when I lived with her, he was here, but not her. I wonder where she is.

I still think she's here sometimes, especially when Ralph's person speaks, but I look up to check who it is less often these days, because it's been so long since the old woman was here. It is all really quite a strange thing that she would disappear like that.

Even though the old woman is not around, I do like living here—as long as I get my own way, that is! Everyone is quite nice to me, even pointy-faced Peggy.

We recently had new toys to play with, which gave Peggy even more soft toys to carry around and be possessive over. I just let her take the soft ones, though, as I prefer the hard rubbery ones. She can have any toy she wants as long as she leaves those ones alone—especially my very own hard rubber toy—if she even dares to touch that, there'll be trouble.

Saturday January 24th

An Early Spring?

Clare

Anthony's four week Christmas break is over and it is time for him to return to university. He has spent much of the time here working; always with Peggy at his side. Once again, after having this time together, they are going to be parted. When he's home we don't change any of the normal dog sleeping arrangements, all three of the dogs continue to sleep in mine and Bob's room. Peggy and Ralph sleep in their own beds and, of course, Lucy sleeps on our bed—what would you expect from a terrier?

We're so grateful when Martin comes to stay every other weekend, because this is when Lucy insists on going and staying in his room for a sleepover. She's quite adaptable and isn't too perturbed about where she sleeps—just so long as she's on a human bed! With Peggy, she's such a sensitive soul that I think it would be detrimental to her to sleep in with Anthony when he's home—she would miss him even more each time he goes away.

The snowdrops are already defying the seasonal weather and decorating the ground with fine, green shoots, and tiny, white petals. Just last week daffodil leaves had begun to push their way through the hard, frozen earth.

Mum would've loved to have seen those subtle promises of spring. She hated January, but the snowdrops, crocuses, and daffodils rearing their heads in the early months of each year, lightened the dark days of winter. Likewise, when the winter solstice was over, she looked forward to the days becoming longer; to the times when she could sit in the park with Lucy and watch the children playing on their skateboards and bicycles. When the weather was warmer she could linger and chat to the other people who were out walking their dogs.

In the last year or so before she died she had struggled to hold onto Lucy's lead, so Martin or I would always walk Lucy. It was mostly Martin because he saw Mum each day, whereas I was only there at weekends. It must have been difficult for Lucy and Martin, because when they lost Mum, essentially they also lost each other. Martin would have had Lucy—he loves her—but he's on kidney dialysis and doesn't walk so well due to severe arthritis and, well, we already had two dogs—we may as well have three. Martin comes to stay on alternate weekends, apparently to see us, but I think it is mostly to see Lucy. Lucy loves him and can hardly contain her excitement when he walks through the door.

Friday January 30th

More Snow

Clare

The snow has arrived with a vengeance and covered the daffodil leaves—there are just one or two still bravely flaunting their greenness through the vast white coat on the ground. The winter feels as though it's going on forever.

The dogs are expressing equal amounts of joy and disdain at the sight of the snow: joy at the opportunity to play and chase snowballs, and disdain because even if it is actually snowing, they still have to go for a walk. Unless she is absolutely desperate, Peggy refuses to go to the toilet in the back garden, hence we walk the three of them three times a day. Lucy, too, prefers to go to the toilet when she's out for a walk. So, come rain, shine, or blizzard, we're out there walking. Lately there have been far more blizzard-like conditions than any of us would have liked to have experienced. There is a line, though, and a few times lately when we haven't been able to venture far; that line has meant that Peggy has had to admit defeat and go to the toilet in the garden.

Ralph quite happily goes to the toilet out the back, and just as Peggy and Lucy have to be desperate to go in the garden, he has to be desperate to go when he's out for a walk. I've often wondered whether it's because of his nervousness, in that he doesn't like to draw attention to himself when he is in a public place. Perhaps it's because he feels exposed, and going to the toilet is a time when if you are a wild creature you are vulnerable to being attacked. I know dogs have come a long way from the days of their ancestor the wolf, but it is possible that such a survival-related instinct is still inherently embedded in our domesticated dogs.

Ralph is getting braver little by little and he's developed a cheeky personality. He playfully makes us chase him around the house, play-bowing whenever we nearly catch him. He likes to sit calmly on the stairs when he has his lead and coat put on to go for a walk. I don't know why he does this; it's just something he decided to do one day. Just now, though, even Ralph who loves his walks seems relieved to not have to go out and brave the elements on a proper walk.

As I write this, the sky is full of much more snow, and the blackbirds and a robin are competing for some bird food I've put on a tray outside. I would normally have scattered it on the grass to enable them to forage, but foraging in four inches of snow can't be easy when your beak is less than half an inch long.

The dogs tolerate the birds in a way they don't tolerate other animals. Ralph will occasionally chase one of the wood pigeons, but he does that far less frequently these days. I think he's realized it's a wasted expenditure of energy to chase birds that immediately launch themselves into the sky as soon as he makes it obvious he's interested in them. He'll still chase the occasional brave rabbit that has dared to venture into the garden, or the odd local cat that thinks the garden birds feeding here are worth risking the rage of two long dogs and a terrier.

As time has gone by there have been fewer cats in the back garden and I guess the dogs are the reason why. A black and white one used to come and sit on top of our garden shed, but I haven't seen him since he ventured down onto the ground at the same time Peggy happened to be going into the garden and, well, luckily the cat disappeared over the fence to safety.

Friday February 14th

The Cold and Just, Well, More Stuff to be Bothered About

Lucy

This cold weather is a bit of a bother. Not to Ralph or Snooty Peg. Nooo, not at all!

When that white stuff is lying on the ground, that's when my height provides me with a bit of a disadvantage. I wear a coat, but those things don't properly protect your tummy, and when you're low to the ground, that bit that wraps around your belly and holds your coat in place gets a little damp; sometimes it even gets soaking wet.

Those other two just stride along with their long legs, and they have their jackets wrapped around them as though they don't have a single care in the world. They don't seem to be bothered how deep the white stuff is, and only really seem to mind when the white stuff is actually falling from the sky—and that's only because that's when they get their heads wet. Heads? That's a bit pathetic really when you think about what I have to contend with. I think walks should be banned when the weather is like that—especially for us little ones with short legs.

I suppose I should at least be grateful I have short hair,

though, because I've seen some of those other little dogs from around here wandering along with big balls of that white stuff hanging from their fur. It's not on really—we little dogs need a little justice! Not that I am suddenly joining in solidarity with the other small dogs. No, no, not at all—I still don't like any of them, and I'll still show them my teeth whenever I get the chance. No, it's simply the principle of the thing! Little dogs have rights and all that.

I've recovered from my visit to the dog torturer, but Peggy had to go back because her ears have been bothering her. You'd have thought that because Peggy was the only one being looked at on that occasion that Ralph and I would have been left at home, but no, we had to go in with her anyway—just for the walk. I can think of much better places to go for a walk. It comes back to that idea of little dogs having rights—the veterinarian's clinic is miles from here. Fancy making us walk, especially with my little legs! Those humans are turning into fitness freaks. Why couldn't we just have taken the car? Or they just have taken Peggy?

Being there and not having anything actually done to me made me think about one of my last outings with the old woman. She left me at the clinic, and while I was there it was very stressful and I showed a man my teeth. He didn't stop trying to put the sharp metal object in my skin, so I bit him! As I said, I did warn them all first by showing them my teeth. Very quickly after I'd bitten him, I fell into a deep sleep. When I woke up I had a tooth missing and a sore mouth, which I thought was a bit of an overreaction to what I had done. My remaining teeth were all squeaky clean though. When I got home the old woman mashed up all my foods and hand-fed me—I was so glad to be back home with her.

It's been such a long time since I last saw her. I fear she is never coming back for me. I sometimes long for it to be just the two of us again.

Sunday March 22nd

The Isle of Skye

Clare

The snow in the south of Scotland had eased and those Scottish mountains were calling. The holiday which had been booked what seemed like ages ago was finally upon us. The weather appeared to be showing signs of getting warmer, and so we optimistically made our final plans for our few days on the Isle of Skye. 'Surely it will be getting warmer up north, too,' we thought to ourselves, 'after all, it will soon be spring!'

And so, with the three dogs in tow, and not forgetting my promise to myself to take Lucy to see some mountains, we embarked on the nine hour journey to the northwest of Scotland. I considered taking Mum's ashes, deliberating for some time about whether it would be appropriate to scatter her so far from all of us in a place she had never visited. In the end, common sense prevailed, and I left her neatly stored on top of the sideboard, right beside the television.

When we arrived in Skye, we realized just how naive we had been to have even considered that the weather might be remotely like it was back home. Those three hundred miles represented a stark difference in climate and, as expected for the north of Scotland at that time of year, it was bitterly cold.

Had we stopped to think about it, we'd have delayed our holiday for a couple of months, but we'd crossed the bridge over The Kyle of Lochalsh onto Skye, and were going to make the most of it. We'd hired a tiny, cozy bothy. As we approached the bothy I noticed how the cotton white, snow-threatening skies matched the whitewashed walls of the little cottage.

The bleakness of the surroundings made us wonder again at our decision to go at that time of year, but it had been a long journey with several comfort breaks for dogs and humans, and we were all exhausted. We unloaded our luggage and headed inside. The temptation of making up a real fire, and sitting and gorging ourselves on the ample supply of food we had carried from home, overrode any desire to go off exploring.

For that day anyway.

The three dogs delighted in a box of treats they'd been left as a welcome gift by the owner of the bothy. Not surprisingly, they seemed as happy as we were to spend the remainder of their first day in the wintry gloominess huddling with us beside the fire.

The bothy was so invitingly snug, and we really had to force ourselves to go off exploring. In the end, we didn't venture too far as the journey up there had been a real trial and had made us not want to spend much more time in the car. We took the dogs walking along local pebbly beaches whose cliffs were touching the thick, grey clouds, and where green and orange-brown seaweed tangled around pink and grey stones in rock pools. We struggled against the biting, freezing cold wind as it battered our faces, and we staggered along frozen mud paths which had embedded their way into the bleak, bronzed hills.

For Lucy, as far as we know anyway, it was her first holiday, and we showed her the hills and mountains I had promised to show her. Whether she was impressed or not, I'm not sure, as the jury's still out on whether dogs have that same sense of wonder. It gave me a sense of satisfaction, however, that I had taken her somewhere she had never been, somewhere neither of my parents had ever travelled to, but somewhere I know they would have loved.

There was no television and no Internet and, for us, it was somewhere we could just relax with a good book and the dogs sprawled out at our sides, or heaped beside one another at our feet. They were sometimes panting in front of the log burner, and at other times huddled together on the sofa. At night time once the fire had died down they draped themselves across one another, vying for the warmest spots, as the bedroom was much colder than the rest of the cottage.

All too soon, it was time to come back home, and our hearts sank when we woke up on the morning we were leaving and discovered it had snowed overnight.

Once all our gear was packed into the car, the dogs seemed all too keen to get moving. Perhaps they sensed we were going home; that we were returning to our centrally-heated home and their normal routines. For us, at home we knew that if they needed to go to the toilet and there was eight inches of snow on the ground, they could simply pop into the garden and race back in again before they got too cold—perhaps that's what they, too, were looking forward to. With the holiday cottage not having a dog-safe garden, each toilet excursion had to be associated with a walk—whatever the weather!

Nine hours later, and after some extremely hair-raising moments on the snowy, slippery, icy roads, we were home. We were pleased we had been away, but equally happy and relieved to be safely back in the comfort of our own surroundings.

Home.

There's something about that safe place which is innately satisfying; a survival instinct for warmth and comfort we have inherited from our forebears—something which seems to be necessary for our wellbeing.

The north of Scotland is one of the most beautiful places on our planet, but home is the place I would always rather be. And I think I know of three canines who agree.

Monday March 30th

Holiday in Skye . . . and that darned cold weather!

Peggy

I despise this cold weather we're having, although at least here at home we only have to go out for our normal walks, and then we're back inside where it's nice and warm.

Back in those racing days of mine I lived outside all the time. I used to find the cold weather was hard on me and my racing colleagues. We greyhounds don't have very thick fur—or much fat—to insulate us. No, there's not much to keep us greyhounds warm once the weather turns.

Anyway, back to what's been going on around these parts, and this is really the point I want to make. It would seem the people are not satisfied with the weather around where we live and decided to pack us all up and take us to somewhere even colder. Are they mad? Honestly, I really think they are! It was madness, utter madness!

The vehicle journey was so long, and they kept on stopping because Ralph was doing that thing where he keeps on pretending he wants to go to the toilet and doesn't really. Honestly—how long can a dog possibly sniff the ground or the bushes before deciding it is about time he had a pee? One time we stopped beside a large stretch of water and it was freezing. It really was so very cold—so cold that I don't think I have ever felt cold like that, not even in my running days. But I have to say that that was nothing compared to the cold we felt once we reached our destination.

Anyway, on one of those stops, I was walking along with the man and the little pipsqueak in front of Ralph and his person, and I caught a whiff of a scent by a tree I thought he would like to pee on. To make him hurry up, I immediately turned around and told him with my eyes that that was where he should go. And he completely ignored me and dragged the woman down to some bushes next to the water's edge. He then spent ages, and I do mean ages, sniffing. In the end, he didn't go there, and instead dragged her off to some more bushes. We went back to the vehicle to wait for them until, eventually, they emerged from between some trees with Ralph looking very satisfied with his urinary achievements. *'Thank goodness for that!'* I thought to myself.

When we at last got to our destination, I must admit I was quite impressed. It was very cozy! But when those flames disappeared, it was freezing! I'm not generally prone to huddling up next to Ralph and the little dog, but my goodness, I had to out of necessity! At bedtime the man and Ralph's person covered us with blankets, so even they must have realized it was cold. What on

Earth are they doing taking us camping in the middle of winter? I know it wasn't really camping, because we were in a building, but it was so cold at night we might just as well have been sleeping outdoors. We were so relieved each morning when they switched the flames back on.

They took us sightseeing, which is very nice and all that, but why, oh why, were we going for walks in the freezing cold? We could have just sat in the car and looked out of the windows. There wasn't that much to see anyway. It was quite boring really—just some hills and a lot of old rocks which had some slippery, slimy stuff all over them. I didn't even see any rabbits or other wild creatures. They all had the right idea—they had either flown away somewhere warmer because of the cold, or were hiding themselves away until the warmer weather came. Oh, and then of course there were the freezing cold waves down at the water's edge. For goodness' sake! Really? Who goes to the seaside when it is so bitterly cold?

Apparently *we* do.

I was so relieved when I saw all our things being put back into the car, and I hoped we were going home. The closer we got, the surer I became that later on I would be sleeping in my comfy, warm bed. And I was. As soon as I saw it in all its coziness, I collapsed into it, rolled onto my back, snuggled down into its warmth, put my long legs in the air, and let out a deep, contented sigh.

Friday April 3rd

Winter Really Does Turn to Spring

Clare

The holiday has done us all a lot of good, and those daffodils have continued to bravely rear their heads. The arrival of their greenness protruding from the ground is concealing their promise of seas of yellow. A friend who lost her own mum a few years before I did said that memories are everywhere. They're in an orange and red autumnal afternoon, a rustle of leaves, the rain beating against the window, a walk in a sun-dappled forest, or the simple sound of the telephone ringing at a particular time of the day.

As I observe those daffodils waiting to proudly lift their blooms to the sky, I know Mum would have commented on them; she would have relished their beauty and their anticipated lust for life. My memories of Mum, for those moments, are encased within those daffodils.

It's been ten months now since she left us; very soon it will be a whole year. Every day I think of her, and when I wake each morning there is a sense of emptiness deep in my abdomen. I stay still and wait for the moment to pass; wait to see whether someone will pinch me and then I'll awaken and find that it was all a bad dream. But no pinch comes, and as realization washes over me I gasp, I inhale and take in as much air, as much oxygen, as I can. As reality seeps into my brain I understand that I haven't been living in another universe for all these months, and that she really no longer exists. This happens every morning, and then each night before I fall asleep, I know that when I rouse I shall have to relive the realization that this is now how things are.

The daytime is much easier because there is more to distract me—that's when I try to recall the good times. I know that she would want my memories of her to be the fond and happy ones, just like her appreciation each year that the flowers were letting the world know that our seasonal warmness will soon arrive.

I'm not sure dogs appreciate flowers in the same ways we humans do. They don't seem to anyway, although I do sometimes think Ralph has a particular sense of wonder at the world that exists around him. It's probably less awe, though, and more a part of his survival instinct. If he notices something fluttering in the distance, or something flapping in the breeze, then he generally watches it from afar just to make sure it is no threat to him. We always say his catchphrase is that adage 'caution equals survival'. It is something he lives by and which you can see in so many of his actions. He watches us and all the moves we make. He also notices when things have changed on his walk, and you can see him taking it all in—making a mental note for the next time he passes by.

Lucy and Peggy are much bolder and braver than that;

they're much more gung-ho in their actions. They've always been much more confident; however they both do have their own insecurities. Peggy has her noise phobia and Lucy, well, not surprisingly really with all that has happened to her, she fears being alone.

Mum loved her, and Lucy loved Mum with the whole of her being. Like Ralph does with us, Lucy watched Mum's every move, and marked every glance Mum made in her direction with a matching glance of her own. Sleep was a pastime Lucy couldn't afford to spend too much time on—lest she missed something. But she didn't do this with Mum in a Ralph 'survival' kind of way—more a need to support and to adore.

When you're used to being around large, gentle, lazy dogs who just want to 'be', and who don't necessarily want heaps of attention bestowed on them (just plenty of food, treats, and walks in Peggy's case), then being in the constant company of a dog like Lucy can come as a bit of a shock to the system.

Where before we'd existed in our house, and the two dogs had comfortably existed by our sides, suddenly we had this very much 'in your face', over-exuberant, over-enthusiastic, small dog with a gigantic attitude, watching our every move. She scrutinizes our every movement and every word, and follows us as we shift from room to room. Meanwhile, the other two linger where they are, only getting up if that usage of energy is going to be beneficial in some way. They say terriers are loyal dogs, and she's certainly that. She has a way of looking directly into your eyes as if she's trying to communicate; as though she genuinely cares what happens to you. Like a parent feeling apprehensive about their teenager's plans for the evening, she wants to know where you're going, what you're doing, who you're going to be with, and, I'm sure if she could ask, exactly what time you will be home. I believe that if she could talk, she would also want to know precisely why you're doing whatever you're doing!

I used to wonder how Mum coped with the constant attention bestowed upon her by Lucy. I think that now I understand—not just about Lucy, but also about other dogs like her. There's a sense of flattery in what she does, and what generations of dogs before her have done and continue to do. Their flattery massages our egos, making us feel loved and wanted. It's easy to see why we have made them our closest companions; the affection we receive in return is worth a multitude of times more than the effort we invest in taking care of them.

Wednesday April 8th

Spring Holiday Time at Last

Ralph

Mum is here a lot more at the moment, and I like it when that happens because when it is warm she leaves the doors open and I can get in and out of the house whenever I want, rather than waiting for someone to open the door to let me outside. It's a bit cold at the moment to stay out there for too long, but it's nice that the sun is shining a lot. The only problem with the sun is that when it is shining on my most loved places such as my very own chair, the little dog keeps trying to get there first, and I have to nudge her out of the way.

Yes, it would appear she has taken a bit of a liking for the house's hot spots. Those hot spots change as the day goes on, and I have to move around them in a particular order so I don't miss out on the heat. The little dog is mean, though, because if I happen to be in a deep sleep and don't notice the light has changed and it's time to move to the next sunny spot, when I do finally get there, there she is, all sprawled out as though she hasn't a care in the world. I'm surprised at how much room she takes up when she extends her legs as far as she can so she can take up all the space. I then have to curl myself up into the smallest ball, and if I nudge her too much, out come those teeth of hers!

I thought the little dog would go away after a while, but she's still here. While I used to be quite scared whenever she chased me, now I think it's good fun. Not when she chases me out of the house, though, I still don't really very much appreciate that!

It's the best fun when we go and bark through the fence at the dogs who live next door. When Peggy joins us it can get quite frightening though, because she looks quite fearsome when all the hairs stand up right along her back. She really doesn't like those dogs very much. When she runs, her back feet almost reach her ears— and she's very fast—even I can't keep up with her when she races up and down the fence with her snarling face and her arched back.

Yes, she's definitely not that keen on those two dogs. I'm just glad she likes Lucy and me, or else we would be very worried—especially as we have to share a house with her!

Mum brought an interesting box into the house. It was squeaking and sounded a bit like those creatures that flutter around the garden—the ones that I try to catch but never quite manage to. Anyway, it seems that the box did indeed contain a couple of those fluttering creatures. And I was very interested in them. I like to think I have a certain affinity with other animals and I am very gentle with them. I think Mum thought I was interested in the creatures in a hungry kind of way, and I wasn't, honestly. I just wanted to help to look after them. Peggy was making out she was interested in them and wanted to help too. I wouldn't trust her, though—I've seen what she's like whenever we see those creatures with the pointed ears!

In the end, they put them in the wooden building outside and would go and take food to them. One day, the fluttering creatures disappeared. I think they may have been set free.

Monday May 25th

Time

Clare

Fifty.

Time—it creeps up on you. It makes you question the world, your achievements, and what that future might hold. You feel the clock ticking and are desperate for it to slow down; and then for it to pause while you do the things you always wanted to do.

Do dogs feel that ticking of time? Do they want to relish a moment? Do they want to linger and enjoy what the day has to offer in case that situation, such as the joy of chasing a ball, or lazing under the apple tree, never happens again? In case that moment is their last? Or are they happy to live each moment for itself, oblivious to the tick-tock of the eternal clock? The clock will continue, but we won't, and therein lies the problem.

People say that dogs have that capacity to live for the moment; that they don't worry about the future. I suppose there's no way we can ever truly know for sure whether this is the case. When we go out, however, dogs seem to expect or anticipate our return, so perhaps there is much more of a concept of time embedded in dogs than we humans think.

Mum's now been gone for more than a year. We survived our first Christmas without her, the first anniversary of her passing, and in five days it will be her birthday again. I was expected on her birthday. She always used to say that I arrived five days early just for her, so she would be well enough once her own birthday arrived to show me off to all and sundry. I'm sure she told me that story every year of my life until she died.

Yes, fifty! Another milestone that makes you look back on your life; it makes you reflect on all that you've done, regret the regrets and rejoice in the good times. How is my life now? How will my life be in the future? What will become of us all? And what will happen to the people whom I love the most?

I still have nightmares. The nightmares are infused with memories, but I don't know how much is real and how much is made of stories I have created. When I wake in the middle of the night, there's that feeling of being hit in the stomach, and of fear for the future and regret for the time we didn't have, and now will never have. All those feelings come rushing in, until I feel frozen in one position. I see her face and don't want to believe she's no longer here.

Lucy knows. I am sure she does, because when I am lying there, and Bob is sleeping with soft sounds coming from his mouth and nose, sweet Lucy, she sneaks from my feet to my face and lies there. Gently she takes in my own breath, shares hers, and comforts me.

Just like last year, I don't feel like celebrating my birthday—it can be easier to just forget that time is moving on; to try not to think too much about what the world has left to offer. What have we humans done to the world? What part can I play in making it better? What can one person do to make their life matter? Thinking about it too much can drive you crazy, and it can often be easier to get lost in a film or go for a walk; to just appreciate time with loved ones.

And forget.

I've told friends and family that I shall mark my half-century birthday, that I'll arrange to hire the local independent cinema and show a film. Mum would want me to do something; she wouldn't want me to still be locked in grief. Grief seems so pointless as it will never bring her back. But right now I can't think of anything worse than celebrating my birthday; to have to feign being cheerful and enjoying myself, when right now all I want to do is find solace in my misery.

Wednesday July 8th

Time to Celebrate

Clare

In the end, and after all my doubts, we arranged to show a film at the small local cinema, and then bring everyone back here so the dogs could join in the celebrations.

But which film to show? In preparing for the event, this was the bone of contention which began with my suggesting *The Sound of Music*. This met disappointed looks from both Bob and Anthony. Chancing it (and reminding them it was MY birthday) I progressed to *Mama Mia*—the same expression washed over both their faces. Okay then, racking my brains and thinking I didn't dare suggest *Dirty Dancing,* they decided to offer a little help. Having scoffed at their facetious suggestions of *Fast and Furious*, or the likes of any of the *Conan* films, I optimistically suggested *Paper Moon*; after all, everyone loves a classic! But no, it met the same look of disapproval.

Finally, after exploring old classics, science fiction, adventure, horror, and every which genre we could think of, I settled on four finalists: Monty Python's The Life of Brian (my number one film of all time, but I was worried some people wouldn't find it funny), *Dead Poets Society* (also one of my best-loved films, but perhaps not the happiest choice), *The Lost Boys* (but realized some people might find it a little frightening—after all it is about vampires), and the winner, *The Last of the Mohicans*. Okay, so it, too, is not so cheery, but the music is amazing!

Thankfully our eventual choice of film went down well, and the get together back at our house afterwards was just what we all needed. Ralph, as usual, was the centre of attention. He is a dog of such contradictions and, true to form, he drifted into the centre of the group to watch everyone. Meanwhile, Lucy and Peggy found a succession of people to force their affections onto, and they immersed themselves in the pleasure of a series of caresses of their dog shampoo-scented, shiny, smooth heads and backs.

When you live with dogs you get used to their special scents, it is part of the joy of living with them—snuggling next to them and inhaling their ingrained canine smell. When you have guests over—and a lot of guests who are not familiar with your house's happy dog aromas, some dog shampoo doesn't really go amiss.

And so, as the dogs enjoyed all the extra fuss they were receiving, who was I to give away trade secrets by admitting that actually our dogs don't usually smell quite like that? They don't really appreciate having baths, so we normally only ever bathe them if there's a reason—it's not good to wash the natural oils from their coats. Instead, we brush them regularly to keep their coats nice and healthy.

Personally, I love the scent of dog—I think if you love dogs you sort of have to. It's such a small price to pay for the rewards we reap from spending our lives with them.

Now the party's over, all I have to do now is try to remain in a positive frame of mind, and think about the rest of summer and all that it offers. This will be the second summer without Mum, and I know I have to move on, I really do know that. I just wish I could sleep without the horrors of the night returning every time I close my eyes.

Monday August 10th

Lucy the Champ

Clare

We spent the summer catching up with people we hadn't seen for a while. Was it part of some continuing existential crisis? I don't know, but it reinforced the need to not let friendships drift. The dogs got to catch up with many of our friends too—some of whom have children, and many of whom Lucy had not yet met.

It was during one of these initial meetings that we discovered Lucy has a tolerance towards children that she doesn't express towards older humans and other dogs. There's always a worry with any dog that they won't be good with children, and this is something we'd never properly assessed in Lucy—we'd never really had to. Some friends were visiting from down south, and we warned the adults and the children to just give Lucy (and Ralph for other reasons) some space. If they wanted to pat a dog, then Peggy was definitely the one who would enjoy it!

What happened a few hours later was a demonstration of how easily you can let down your guard. The dogs had been good and the kids had been good. Lucy was sat next to me, and the two of us were sat on cushions on the floor. The other side of me was our eleven-year old Adam. We were all engrossed in conversation and the dogs were lying resting. Suddenly, Adam's elder sister looked beyond me at Adam and declared, 'Adam, you were told to not touch her!'

Looking down at Adam, I realized he was now sitting the other side of me, right next to Lucy, which was fine, but the worrying thing was that he had Lucy's much-loved rubber toy in his hand.

'How did you get that from her?' I asked, without any attempt to hide the sense of alarm in my voice.

'I just took it out of her mouth,' he quite calmly replied, clearly wondering what all the fuss was about.

His sister immediately told him to let Lucy have it back. With a shrug, he offered it back to her, at which Lucy oh so gently took it from him. 'She just let me have it,' he stated defensively, with a shrug of his small shoulders.

My heart was pounding as I realized what could have happened. It was her most-loved toy in the world, and one she would normally have defended to the ends of the Earth, but instead she had demonstrated a gentleness not normally shown to the rest of us. If we go to pick it up, she sometimes warns us with a growl, but this time there had been nothing. Perhaps she knew he was just a young boy, and that behaving in her usual Lucy-way was not acceptable. I suppose it's possible she was in a home with children in her previous life in Ireland? Perhaps she had loved a child? I don't know, but I would never, ever be complacent with her in that way again, even though she had clearly behaved perfectly.

The news is rife with examples of situations that have resulted in children being injured, or even killed, when they've been attacked by dogs. You only have to look at postings of pictures and video clips of children interacting with dogs on social media, however, to see the terrible risks some people take. Those subtle signs that dogs give so freely are often ignored, or not recognized. What can appear to be a happy picture of a child hugging their dog, can be extremely horrifying when you understand the expression on the dog's face: a yawn, a lick of the lips, panting, a lifted paw, ears folded backwards, a sideward glance revealing the white of their eye—these are all signs that tell us to keep away. All the dog often wants (and needs) is some space.

We were lucky with Lucy—we took precautions, but the precautions we had taken in the end may not have been enough. She really was so well-behaved, but the positive outcome is completely down to her, and not to the things we did to avoid problems.

With all our summer visitors safely on their way home, we found time to reflect on what the summer had held for us. The unpredictable climate has brought with it plenty of opportunity for us British to do what we do best, and talk about the weather. Someone Bob knows who is from Spain, said that what he loves most about the British weather, is that you just never know what you are going to find in the morning when you open the curtains. How will the sky be? Will it be blue, grey, orange, red, purple, white, or a mixture of all of these? Every day brings a new surprise. I can absolutely appreciate that, but on those short, wintry days when the sky is mostly dark grey, or full of white snow, how I long for it to be blue with fine, wispy, white clouds threaded through it. Luckily the summer has so far given us plenty of those blue-skied, long, hot, restful days.

Ralph loves those days too. He loves to sunbathe, and Lucy loves to do the same. I love days like today when the two of them vie for the sunniest spots, and they both follow the sunshine as it moves around the house. First the bedroom, then on to the sitting room, and finally the dining room. Once the sun reaches there, the two of them compete for space on the bucket chairs which adorn the two bay windows. Eventually the summer sun disappears from our house, settling in shades of red and mauve behind the trees in the nature reserve over the road.

Peggy, meanwhile, can be found as far from the sun streaming through the house as possible—usually on the landing where it's nice and cool. This happens so often that we've put her a large dog bed at the top of the stairs so she can just wander up there and be comfortable whenever she feels the need to get away from the heat. This also gives her respite from the hustle and bustle of Lucy and Ralph as they keep watch from the dining room windows, searching for dogs, cats, wild rabbits, or the postman to bark at.

Lucy's competitive spirit is not confined to treats or sunny spots in the house. She has been known to try to defend the oddest of things. Just the other day, she even defended a blade of grass that was hanging out of the side of her mouth. Bob pulled out the long, green blade and put it on the ground beside him; only for Lucy to leap on top of it, bare her teeth and growl. That terrier instinct is so strong in this extremely mixed up little dog, and she constantly reminds me of the extra care we have to take with her—despite her recent display of being quite trustworthy!

She's been through so much, and I know that with Mum she was given fairly free rein to give in to her terrier instincts; she was allowed to be that bossy, forthright dog that is in her genes. With us, it is much trickier for her as she does have to be much better behaved. She seems to understand that there are boundaries, whereas her life with Mum had very few; she really did have carte blanche to do whatever she wanted.

Friday September 25th

The Mail

Clare

With Adam, Lucy demonstrated she does have the ability to hold back when she seems to know she has to. But with dogs like Lucy you just have to be that bit more wary; a little more vigilant. We shall always be cautious with her when visitors are over, at least until she is relaxed and has accepted their presence. And we shall never, ever, allow her to come into contact with the postman.

Ralph, though, likes the postman or, rather, he likes the post—so much that if he sees it fall from the letter box, he tears it open. Bob, always striving to be several steps ahead of the dogs' antics, decided he would import the 'great solution to the problem' from America for ten dollars.

'This will fix it,' he declared to anyone who was listening, while he satisfyingly secured what was essentially a bag with toughened studs along its edges to the inside of the front door. The concept was simple—the post would simply fall into the bag, and said dog(s) would never know the letters were there.

Once he had finished attaching it to the door, with screwdriver still in hand, he stood up and admired his handiwork. Meanwhile, inside I had my doubts—doubts which bubbled to the surface and were substantiated the following day as I opened the front door after a few hours' absence. There, hanging from the door, was our nice new post bag. Unfortunately, however, it was completely ripped down its seam. Beneath it lay the mail—admittedly a little less damaged than usual as the bag had clearly provided a new pastime, but there was definitely some tell-tale Ralph saliva (no DNA test required) and a few tooth marks on each of the letters.

Not believing it was necessary to get in touch with the company to tell them their dog-proof mail-bag was certainly not Ralph-proof, Bob felt energized by the concept, and decided he would make one of his own. And so, late one evening a few days ago, he determinedly fitted a hessian supermarket bag to the inside of the door—just underneath the letterbox.

The amazing thing is that so far it has worked. Over the last few days the post has waited for us nestled safely inside the supermarket bag. For a supermarket bag it is thankfully quite attractive and has a green tree adorning its front. The potential is still there for Ralph to tear it down, but perhaps over time he will lose interest in the post—apart from the occasional anticipated bout of misconduct. I suspect one reason it may have worked, however, is the texture of the material, which probably isn't the nicest to chew.

Friday October 16th

The Post and Other Amusements

Ralph

I used to love it when exciting things would drop onto the mat through the hole in the front door. All those bits of paper would smell different to one another—some of them would smell of tasty food, sometimes interesting people, occasionally other dogs, or even those creatures with the pointed ears.

Each morning I would sit in my own special, comfy chair, and watch through the window for the man who would come and put the bits of paper through the door. If I nodded off, I would still get there in time for the papers to drop, because I would wake up when I heard the clink of the front gate. If, on the rare occasion I missed him, usually because Mum had left the speaking box on too loud, I still occasionally heard the papers actually falling to the floor.

Once the papers had been delivered, I would race through there and scatter the paper around the hall. What was the best fun was to fling them around, chew the edges of them, and spit the bits out on the floor. This was because, while they did smell quite interesting, they didn't taste so good.

I can't have this fun anymore. I still see or hear the man

coming to the door, but the papers no longer fall on the floor, but disappear into some strange kind of bag. I tried pulling the bag, but it doesn't taste very good.

Anyway because of all this, when Mum goes out I've had to return to the old ways I had of amusing myself. This is when I go around the house collecting anything that belongs to her, and then I leave them all in the hallway for when she comes back. I think she likes me doing that, because when she returns she tells me 'Good Boy,' and then she goes and puts them back where I found them. It's quite a good game really—I think she prefers me playing that game to the one where I rip the paper that comes through the door.

Peggy and the little dog are a bit boring, especially Peggy. Whenever Mum and the man are out she goes and lies upstairs. At least the little dog sometimes comes and stands next to me while we bark at the people who are walking past the house. I think she thinks she is scaring them away, but I think she's delusional. I know it's me they're frightened of.

Saturday December 10th

Twinkling Lights and Stupid Big Dogs

Lucy

A tree with lights that twinkle at night time has again appeared in the room in which the humans watch the box in the corner and we all relax. The tree reminds me of days long ago—of things that happened in the past. Some of the smells remind me of the old woman, and times when I would sit next to her and protect her. I don't remember her so well now. I haven't seen her for so long. The last time I saw her I was very frightened, but now here I am living with Ralph and pointy-faced Peg—and they're not so bad really. At least, I suppose they're not that bad when they're not making me cross!

Ralph really does have moments when it seems as though he goes out of his way to annoy me. And he can be a bit stupid sometimes. Take the man who brings the bits of paper and puts them through the letter box. He still brings the bits of paper, but when he puts them through the door, Ralph doesn't seem to realize they're falling into that bag contraption which the man has put on the inside of the door. It is so obvious! I am tiny, but I know, even though I can't actually see inside the bag. Ralph is big enough to see, but he hasn't even got the sense to look. These large dogs really aren't very intelligent! Although, I have to say that Peggy knows they are there, but she simply isn't interested in such things. She is only ever interested in something if it has food associated with it.

Instead of spending his time waiting for bits of paper to land on the floor, now Ralph spends his time parading around the house as though he owns it, gathering all the things together that belong to his person. I follow him, and occasionally growl at him to get him to behave, but he won't. He just stays focused on collecting those things and then leaves them in a heap by the front door.

Peggy never gets involved, she simply goes and lies at the top of the stairs, and every now and then I hear her let out a deep sigh. Once Ralph has finished collecting, he goes and stands by the front window and waits for people to go past. The two of us have the occasional barking competition if we see another dog through the window, but not Peggy—she continues to lie at the top of the stairs sighing to herself.

Recently there've been a lot of visitors. I always go to the door and check them out to make sure I'm happy for them to be allowed inside. Once they're in, I stand right next to them and stare at them until I'm sure they are behaving themselves. If Ralph or Peggy try to get any attention from them, I glare at them too. I'll have none of that attention-seeking behaviour! No, I just tell them with my eyes they had better not dare get involved! No, the visitors are mine to sort out.

2016

Saturday January 23rd

Norv and Bandit

Clare

Another New Year.

Twelve more months have passed, and it's time to wave cheerio, farewell, auf Weidersehen, au revoir, adios, to the last year and all its highs and lows.

Mum hated New Year. She loved Christmas and all the festivities, but while many are sometimes relieved to put the previous year behind them and move on to a fresh start, I guess that for Mum what had passed was a known entity; she had dealt with it. The New Year, however, would present new challenges and unexpected events. I think it was those unexpected events that bothered her, because she really had seen so much heartbreak. And so, when each New Year came along, she would take her hot water bottle and go to bed, treating the new day as an extension of the previous one.

You never know what's to come, though, do you? You can never tell what the next twelve months will hold. I guess I have inherited some of Mum's sentiments about this. Perhaps it would be better if we didn't count time in years, but in seasons, and in a much more linear way where there is no marking of the end or beginning of another year. Just a life? Perhaps that's what we should have as markers, just the beginning and the end?

This New Year we are host to a couple of extra creatures to keep ourselves distracted: Norv, short for Rattus norvegicus, and his dumbo-eared rat brother, Bandit, have come to stay while their owner is on holiday in Australia for five weeks. To our knowledge, because you never really know for sure with rescue dogs, none of the dogs have ever before encountered pet rats. I'm sure they've seen the odd sewer or river rat lurking around from time to time, but not this domesticated type. Ralph and Peggy had been around when we had our hamster, Mr. Chan, but rats are a bit of a different entity.

I say that Norv and Bandit are brothers, but with the two of them being rehomed creatures, just as it is with our dogs, their history is a little murky. The rats were acquired as part of a group of five, and the other three have gradually died off. These two were the only two who had larger than normal 'dumbo' ears, so it's always been assumed they are related. They are quite bonded to one another, so it's possible the assumption is correct.

A long time ago we had rats of our own, and the dogs

(of the time) were completely happy for the rats to run along the sofa while they were lying on it. Sometimes the rats would snuggle up next to the dogs, and they would all relax together. With Norv and Bandit being only a temporary arrangement, however, we decided it wasn't worth trying to socialize the dogs with them.

Unfortunately, the dogs had other ideas.

As we tried to settle the rats into the spare bedroom, Lucy was snuffling under the door, desperately attempting to get some inkling of what we were doing. The worry for us was that with her being a terrier, her interest might have been more than simple inquisitiveness. As I recalled images I've seen of mid-1800s rat-catcher Jack Black with his Lucy-like terrier at his side, I decided that Lucy would never be allowed to go into the 'rat' room. It was out of bounds!

A few days after settling Norv and Bandit into their temporary surroundings, Ralph, who had seemed a little oblivious to all the goings-on, decided it was time to see where the bits of food making their way upstairs were going. Rightly or wrongly, I trustingly went against my initial reservations and decided to let him and Peggy see what was in the room. Peggy seemed disinterested, or was feigning disinterest, as dogs and cats sometimes do. I did at one point see a forward flick of her ears, revealing her racing tattoo, which with her normally folded ears usually stays hidden. Meanwhile, Lucy, when my determined mission to make the rat-room out of bounds guard was down, clambered up onto the bed so she could see directly into the rats' enclosure. Ralph? Well, Ralph looked as though his eyes were going to pop out of his head! He offered soft whimpers in the back of his throat and put his ears forward. Was this in a hunting way? I'm not sure!

Surely not Ralph? My dear, sweet, gentle Ralph wouldn't hurt a fly!

Whatever the case, and even though these rats are dog-savvy, I decided it was too risky to allow any of the dogs further access to the room, and they were all banished; until further notice they were authorized to only roam the rest of the house. The rat room was definitely out of bounds—even when humans were present!

Sunday January 31st

The Creatures in The Room

Peggy

Some creatures came to stay. The first thing I knew about it was when I noticed food was disappearing into one of the upstairs rooms.

When I secretly sniffed under the door, I could smell something that was curiously like a small creature who used to live in the tall one's room. That creature was a weird animal—he used to stuff his face full of food. Hide it, he did, right there in his face!

Eventually, Ralph's person allowed us in there for a look, and whoa, my giddy aunt, there were two creatures in there! Greyhounds are clever by the way, we can count! When we chase that furry thing around the track there is clearly only one of them, and this was very obviously more than that—one for me and one for Ralph. Anyway, there were indeed two of those creatures, one dark and one light, and both had very pointed faces and long, twitching whiskers. They were also much larger than that sneaky face-filling creature had been! They had the thinnest, longest tails, which they didn't seem to be wagging very much.

I couldn't help myself, I wondered what they would taste like and licked my lips, but then when I whimpered and put my ears up, I was very quickly ejected from the room—closely followed by Ralph.

Shortly after this, the little dog managed to get into the room when Ralph's person was opening the door, but Ralph's person quickly made it clear she was not allowed in there. Quite horrified at this injustice, the little dog and I lay outside the door and wondered why Ralph's person was talking so nicely to those pointy-faced creatures.

I think people are just spoilsports—just one lick of one of those creatures would have been enough for me—and I'm sure they wouldn't mind. I think Ralph's person doesn't trust me because I've noticed there's been some sort of contraption put on the outside of the door to make it more difficult to open. Not that I would, of course. You can trust a greyhound's word, really you can, although I wouldn't be too sure about trusting the little dog's word.

Friday February 26th

Rats, Old Ladies, and Dogs

Clare

In the end, the rats' stay passed with Norv and Bandit remaining securely intact. I used to worry about them—worry I was entertaining them enough. I probably gave them too many treats, and would scour the pet store looking for extra fun things for them to do, and cut branches from our fruit trees to adorn their pen. At nights I'd go into the spare room and let them have a good run around. But even with all that I didn't feel it was enough; rats are such intelligent creatures. I loved having them stay. I don't like the thought of animals being in cages, however, and I think that's probably why their rat-mum asked me to look after them; she shares that sentiment.

The dogs certainly seemed to envy all the attention being bestowed on the contents of that one room. If dogs feel envy, that is, which I think they do. You only have to be stroking one dog, to hear the sighs, and see the facial expression of the other dog across the room, to know they feel something akin to what we would describe as envy.

There was a massive quantity of food and a lot of consideration being invested in that room for those five weeks. I'm sure all three dogs were relieved when they realized that the rats were on their way home, and they could at last return to receiving all of our undivided attention.

Lucy's been with us now for almost two years. That time has flown, but she has become an integral part of our lives. We would never want to be without her. I don't know whether she still thinks about and longs for Mum to still be here. I know I do—every day. I see her everywhere, and often have to do a double-take.

Parking up at the supermarket today, my heart lurched when I saw a lady walking about ten yards from my car with her back to me. On second glance, and when I saw her profile, apart from her hair she was not at all like Mum. There have been other women who have looked far more like her.

I didn't notice before how many old ladies walk just like she did, wear clothes like she used to wear, and carry the type of handbag she used to carry. She would wear it over her shoulder, but would grip it tightly so no one could grab it and run off with it. And when you start to notice things like that, you see that other women do it too, just as she used to. Mum was sure there were pickpockets everywhere, lurking and waiting to jump out at her, and so she made it her mission to constantly protect herself from those desperate thieves. Much later on in life, and certainly for the two or three years before she died, she wore a bum bag she asked me to buy for her online. With her new-found friend the bum bag, she could keep all her worldly goods stashed around her middle. That way she didn't need to worry so much about someone grabbing her shoulder bag. There was nothing of value in the bag—it was simply put there as a decoy.

Those small old ladies with shortish, dark, wavy hair—they seem to be everywhere. I know there are many old ladies, especially with our ageing population—but ladies like her who have retained much of their hair colour, I see so many of them just like Mum. They are all women who are nowhere near ready to die. I don't think she was either. When I see these ladies my heart lurches, and a dull realization washes over me. I don't resent in any way those old ladies with their hair and handbags; I just wish that Mum was still one of them. I wish that she was walking beside me in the aisles of the supermarket, and deliberating over cans of baked beans.

The week before Mum died I was driving to see her, and I can remember thinking that we would still have many more years together. Even at that thought, I felt there were too few for us to be able to share, and that we had to make each one special; make each day that we were together special; make each phone call one that mattered. Why did I have that thought? Why was I even thinking something so morbid?

That last Sunday when I visited her, once we had been to the supermarket for her weekly shop, I took her for a drive around the streets to look at all the spring blossom on the trees. Although she lived opposite a park, she found it difficult to walk as far as the benches to sit down. Because of this I used to drive her to the other side of the park where the trees were, and where she could walk to a bench and sit and take in the scents of the flowers. Sitting there she could watch everyone else who was out with their dogs. Meanwhile, Lucy would do her usual bossy growling at all and sundry, and Mum would apologize to the other people and tell them Lucy didn't like other dogs.

That last day we didn't go to the park. Mum said the drive out had been enough for her. So after I put her shopping away, Lucy and I walked to the park and had a good run along the man-made tarmac paths and between all the trees. The park is on a hill, and as we wandered between the trees I chatted to Lucy, and laughed at her antics as she strutted around as though she owned the place. Little did I know that just a week later this crazy, mixed-up dog would be living in my house.

Mum looked a lot like the Queen—I often thought that about her, but I don't think I ever told her. I said to Bob the other day that I thought Mum had looked a lot like the Queen, and he agreed. I wish I had told her, I think she would have liked that. She loved the Queen.

I wonder whether, like I do, Lucy sometimes sees women who look like Mum did, and whether she also has that moment where she wants to run over and greet them. Lucy's sight is failing, though, but with dogs' predominant sense being that of smell, every now and then she will catch the scent of something, and she will sniff at it more enthusiastically than usual. It makes me wonder whether sometimes those smells remind her of her life before she came to be with us.

The life she had with Mum.

As I've said before, on so many occasions Mum made me promise that should anything happen to her, I would have Lucy. She loved animals and hated the idea of her ending up with someone who would treat her badly—she was adamant that she didn't want her rehomed outside of the family. One of Mum's pet hates was dog crates, and she frequently said she didn't ever want Lucy to be subjected to having to be in a crate. I share Mum's disdain for crates. She knew Lucy would be safe with me, and that I would bring her into my home and she would never, like so many dogs, have to spend time in a cage. She would be a proper part of our family.

A crate really is a cage, and there are no fancy ways of wrapping that up. If a tiger were to spend any length of time in a cage of the same proportions compared to its body size, there would be outrage. So why has it become such common, and seemingly acceptable, practice for dogs to be left in these wire cages? I fear it is convenience, laziness, and a complete lack of understanding of animals' needs.

People have such busy lives these days that there doesn't seem to be the time or the inclination to properly housetrain a dog, or get him used to a little down time so he feels comfortable in his own environment. Instead, so often the dog is conveniently (for the owner anyway) stored in a cage while they go out to work.

I know the theory of crates, and I get that, I really do — they are intended to give the animal a safe place to go to; somewhere that feels as though it is their own. It can be a way of getting them used to travel crates, if these are going to be used. What a lot of people don't realize, however, is that they were originally intended to be somewhere for a dog to go *voluntarily*, with the door left open, not somewhere they are placed with the door closed for their owner's convenience. There is something fundamentally wrong with using them like that. At what point in our relationship with dogs, did we ever deem it acceptable to shut a dog away like that?

I've heard such terrible horror stories from people who have quite voluntarily offered their tales of woe about their dog's situation. They tell of their dogs with separation anxiety who they put in the crate while they go to work for eight or nine hours—and this is all to prevent the dog from chewing the furniture. So, you take an already stressed dog and put him in a box to prevent him from being stressed. This just absolutely does not make any sense.

I heard of a dog who had separation anxiety who, while his owner was away, would howl all the time he was in the cage. Another dog who managed to escape from a cage was subsequently padlocked inside the cage to prevent him from chewing his way out. Yet another dog was urinating in his cage while left at home all day, and his owner couldn't see why this situation was unacceptable. I never told Mum these stories, for I knew it would definitely have stopped her from sleeping. She used to worry so much about such things. I just reassured her that Lucy would absolutely come to live with us if ever the worst happened. Which, of course, it did.

A lot of dogs that end up in rescue have experienced crate cruelty in their previous home, and then misguided people advise the new owners to put the dog in a crate to provide him somewhere to use as a den, often not realizing the new owner will interpret this as being permission to store the dog in the crate while they go to work. Whenever I see crates for sale in the local newspaper, my heart sinks.

The dog who was urinating in his crate must have gone mad waiting all day for his owner to come home. There was no dog walker, no one popping home to see him and let him out to the toilet. How many people would be able to hold on for nine or ten hours? So why do they expect their dog to?

Mum was often quite wise in much of her thinking about the world, and used to discourage people she met from using a cage. She and Lucy used to live opposite a park, and if ever anyone who stopped to talk to her mentioned crates, Mum would enter her anti-crate rhetoric. I don't have that directness she had, and if I hear of someone using one I will hold back a little and try to diplomatically suggest alternatives.

Many dogs do feel separation anxiety, even apparently confident little dogs like Lucy. She never chewed anything, which is often a sign of separation anxiety, but she clearly had worries which made her not want to be alone. To begin with she struggled, and would try not to let us out of her sight. I think having the other dogs here has helped her. In fact, I'm sure it has—dogs love company, be that human or canine company. Even Lucy, I think, now appreciates her canine companions.

Giving a dog something that smells of the human they are missing can also help in this situation, and this is something dog people have known and practiced for decades. When settling in new puppies, kittens or older animals into the family, for example, something from their previous surroundings can allow them a little comfort when adapting to their new environment.

While much of Mum's stuff is now in our loft, I keep a box of her things in our office. Even though nearly two years have passed, they must still smell of her and the flat where she and Lucy lived together. When Lucy came to live with us I gave her a soft, blue and purple scarf of Mum's. She still has it in her bed in our bedroom, but I am sure that after repeated necessary cycles in the washing machine with all the other dog bedding, the scent on that is now long gone.

Lucy's bed, hmm! It very quickly became apparent that sweet little Lucy likes her creature comforts! She'd been used to sleeping on Mum's bed. This was after Mum had tried to get her to sleep in her own dog bed on the floor beside her own bed. Lucy was not having any of it, and that dog bed ended up being the one I would have in my car for whenever Lucy was coming out with us.

Being aware of this keenness for human beds meant I was a little ahead of Lucy in the game regarding her sleeping arrangements. So, that first bedtime, we pointedly showed Lucy where she was to sleep. It was pretty obvious to all, as it was right next to the other two—all three dog beds were nicely lined up and size-related—two large and one small.

And it worked.

For a while it did anyway, but for a long time now she's made alternative arrangements to the bed offered to her.

Our alarm normally goes off at six, and one night after she'd been with us for a few months, Lucy jumped up onto the bed when we were just in those last throes of sleep and anticipating the radio coming on. Not being that good in the mornings until we've got up and started moving around, we only half-heartedly sent her back to her own bed. We drifted off to sleep to try and catch those last few precious moments of slumber, at which Lucy jumped back up and received no resistance. Realizing she was winning, gradually she began to join us on the human bed earlier and earlier during the night and early hours of the morning.

We noticed she had taken a liking to Peggy's large bed and so, even though she had her own Lucy-sized bed, optimistically, we bought her one the same as Peggy and Ralph's two beds—a nice, big, greyhound-sized bed. We knew it was ridiculously big for her, but hoped she would use it. Not surprisingly, no way was she going to sleep in it, so we now have three large dog beds in the bedroom and only two of them are ever occupied!

Now at bed time all she waits for is to have her night time biscuits in her bed and then, up she jumps, right on top of the duvet! Battle over: Humans—nil; Lucy—wins forever more.

Some might say we're being too soft on her, but she's had it tough so a little extra comfort goes a long way. Our friends have a large Labrador, Ava, tucked up each night on their bed, and our old lurcher Jack used to lie alongside me—little Lucy is only about a quarter of Ava and Jack's size. And, after all, dogs have been sleeping alongside humans for millennia.

Saturday April 2nd

What to Do?

Clare

While writing helps in a cathartic way to rid my mind of regrets and jumbled up memories, grief can sometimes take on a life of its own. I know I am incredibly lucky to have such a supportive and wonderful husband and son—I know that, and it makes me feel guilty that I sometimes seem to wallow in self pity. But, as ever, the two of them and my three dogs provide me with the strength I need to get through some of the darkest days.

While all around me life seems to be normal, inside there's still this incredible turmoil. Along the way, the dogs have been here, demonstrating their apparent understanding of how I am feeling, and further enforcing why our two species have forged this incredible human-animal bond.

A year after Mum died, during my routine kidney transplant checkup, I had sat in the clinic sobbing about nothing in particular. This, coupled with my extremely low mood, resulted in a referral to the psychiatry department—to the waiting list anyway. My consultant did advise, however, that although grief varies in how it affects each of us, many people will have found a degree of acceptance after fifteen months or so.

Ok, I thought on leaving the hospital at the time, fifteen months, just three months away. Despite the fact that by fifteen months I may have regained some kind of 'acceptance', the referral to psychiatry went through anyway, mostly because I was still feeling so awful. I was feeling as though I was on a rollercoaster ride and there was no easy way to get off.

In the UK we can be plagued with long waiting lists to see specialists, and after another three months had passed, and I realized that was, indeed, my fifteen months up, I felt a little lifted, as though I had made progress. Perhaps the slight lift in mood was psychosomatic, I don't know.

While I had been writing, working hard at work, and juggling the emotions of this little dog who, to be honest, seemed to have settled in well, all along there had been an elephant in the room: Mum's ashes.

I've heard people say that doing whatever they decided to do with their loved one's ashes has helped their own recovery.

But ashes are a problem—human ashes. What *do* you do with them? Where do you put them? There's a much-loved place like a beach, a mountain, or a forest. There's a nice wooden urn which you can use as an ornament, or perhaps you could choose internment in their own or someone else's grave. You can have your loved one made into jewellery and wear them around your neck, or put some of their ashes into a locket. You can put them in a photograph frame. As I browsed the Internet searching for inspiration, I realized the possibilities appeared to be endless.

Yes, it would appear that where ashes are concerned, the sky's the limit. Indeed, I've even heard of people blasting their loved one's ashes into the sky on a small rocket.

Or, you can perhaps leave those ashes in their green plastic urn next to the television, and spend a whole year or more looking at them. That's what I did. That was all except for a journey during which we took the ashes to Birmingham. At the time I had some vague notion that we would scatter her down there on my grandfather's grave. In the end, though, it didn't feel right—or maybe I just wasn't ready to let her go. So she came back to the space beside the TV and we carried on looking at her, wondering what on Earth we were going to do. She never said what she wanted to have done with her ashes; she didn't even say she wanted to be cremated—that was our decision—and the method chosen because that's what she had done with my dad. So, for several more months, we continued to gaze at that green urn.

I bought her flowers and stood them next to the urn. And then, because the flowers would inevitably wilt and die, I bought her a plant. In the end, more than a year had gone by, and in a moment of what I thought was genius, I moved her ashes from beside the TV, and put the urn inside a large plant pot on the patio. I then planted some lavender on top of her. I'm not so sure she liked lavender! She always used to say it reminded her of old ladies. At the point when she died, I suppose she had been an old lady, so I imagined she wouldn't mind any more.

And so, she has stayed there, and each time I open the curtains she is out there—and I consider what on Earth I am going to do with her. I read that some people plant their loved one's ashes in the back garden, and then shortly after I heard that, I heard the same thing on a radio show. I guess that is sort of what I have done but without the same degree of permanence. I don't plan to leave her there forever—just while I think about what I should do and where I should put her. I guess I'm frightened that if ever we move house, and I have perhaps created a special memorial garden, that I would have to exhume her ashes. At least this way we can lift the pot and move her with us.

I know people who keep their loved one's ashes under the bed or on top of the wardrobe. In many ways what I have done is no different, and where she is I can talk to her and remember her whenever I am out there gardening. In winter I can always see the pot through the French windows. In the days when everyone was buried, there was that sense of completion, and somewhere to go when you were missing them or wanted to talk to them. I guess I created that too, only there is no gravestone, just a glazed, blue plant pot and some lavender for me to chat to.

I was shocked the first time I saw Ralph cock his leg up against the pot, but then I thought about it for a while, and I think Mum would have approved. She would have had that infectious belly laugh she sometimes had, and through tears of laughter would have asked me why on Earth I had put her in a big blue pot, against which Ralph could relieve himself. In the end, it's no different to a gravestone—I've seen plenty of dogs visiting cemeteries with their owners, and I'm sure many of those dogs are prone to the occasional crafty lift of the leg. Having said that, though, I've now moved the pot to a part of the patio where it's protected from Ralph being tempted to lift his leg. It seemed right to move it.

The men with whom I share my life: husband, son and brother, continue to say the same thing, '*You do what you want to do with the ashes; whatever you think is right.*' It seems that, whether I signed up for it or not, the decision has been left to me. She didn't say, though! She didn't say where (or even whether) she would want to be scattered.

Martin and I tried talking to her before she died about whether she had recorded her wishes anywhere, but she thought it was all a bit morbid. So the conversations never happened.

We had had conversations about her being an organ

donor, and she had been so for fifty years or more, but when you die of an infection, which is what she did, understandably no one really wants your organs. This one final act, which we know for sure she would have wanted to have given to the world, she was not able to. A tiny organism had infiltrated Mum's respiratory system, multiplied and beat her multi-cellular body into submission, until finally the power of the effects of that infection were too much her to take. The sheer efficiency of these viral beings had, in a matter of days, stolen the essence of her.

Sunday April 10th

Grief and the Power of Dogs

Clare

A series of what would appear to have been administrative errors in the psychology department resulted in my never receiving grief counseling. A year had passed by since referral, and still I had not seen a psychiatrist. Eventually there came a point when I just realized that the only one who could help me, the only one who could get me out of this deep, desperate rut, was me.

Grief is a strange thing. Whether you're human or canine, depending on the strength of your relationship with that person or animal, you do appear to eventually go through some kind of process which allows you to heal. In the end, your responsibilities in life, the things you have to do every day, those are the things that help you to get through. In our case, the dogs made a huge contribution to that process. The dogs needed to be walked and fed, they needed us to give them our attention; to consider them in everything we were doing . . . and chat to them. The healing power of dogs has become such an integral, and probably accidental, part of the relationship we, as humans, have with them.

Ralph, Peggy and Lucy, they're here. They're in my midst when there's no one else around. They demonstrate a degree of seemingly heartfelt, relentless affection. They listen to my ramblings, and they love; just love; seemingly loving me unconditionally. That unconditional love is something I have been so grateful for in my lowest moments in the time since Mum died. You wonder how you can ever repay dogs for the affection they give—how you can ever give back to them the abundant amount of comfort they've provided you with every second of every day.

This bond between dogs and humans is unique. Whether it began because they were helping people to hunt, or whether it has always been solely for companionship, it doesn't matter, because across many millennia since that bond was forged, the relationship we have with them has become robust.

As people in receipt of this affection, I feel we need to reciprocate, but perhaps to do so properly we need to attempt to delve into the recesses of the dog's mind, and truly, anthropomorphically, put ourselves in their position. Perhaps we should ask how we would feel if we were living the life they live. If we think their life is in any way negative, then we should make their life better. We should consider whether we would be comfortable, well-fed, and mentally fulfilled. If *they* could communicate with us verbally, I wonder what they would say. I only know that I'm forever in my own dogs' debt for the support they give, and I want to make their lives as happy as I possibly can.

Saturday April 16th

Time, Time, Time . . . and More on the Power of Dogs

Clare

Time is moving on.

Mum has been gone for almost two years. For a long time I resented the fact that she died without warning. How dare she leave us? How dare she give up like that? Why would she die without fighting more? Why did she not phone us, so we could have battered down the doors and got her some medical help which might have saved her? How could she leave Lucy, after promising she would be there for her? How dare she go without saying goodbye?

Mum was seventy four years old when she died. She got her three score years and ten, and then some. Not so long ago this would have been described as a 'good innings'. A 'good lot'. Not so anymore. People are still young at seventy. Some people are still climbing mountains at eighty, going to exercise classes at ninety, or dancing at a hundred years of age. In my darkest hours, I think she gave up. I think she knew that night that she could be dying, and in spite of Lucy being there with her, she had no inclination to do anything to try to save herself. In my more rational hours, I believe she simply had no energy; that perhaps her flu medication had knocked her out and that if she could have, she would have phoned—she would have called one of us to go and try to help her. In my heart, I know she wouldn't have chosen to have left us all—she wouldn't have wanted to have left her little dog. I get some comfort from knowing she wasn't alone in those final hours but, conversely, I know how dreadful it must have been for Lucy.

I admire dogs, though. I admire them for their seemingly seamless ability to forgive; for the ways in which they bear no grudge and appear to just love.

Less so as time has gone by, but certainly in the early months when she arrived with us, Lucy used to have what appeared to be very stressful dreams. We would immediately wake her and remind her where she was, and that she was now okay—all those nightmares were in the past. These were similar to the nightmares which Ralph had when we first brought him to live with us. I am sure that, just as we sometimes do, dogs relive their past traumas in their sleep.

As Lucy has become more accepting of her new situation, time has begun to heal and I, too, have been able to put things into perspective and get on with life. It is still very early days and it is difficult, but I understand why so many people I know who have been through the same sort of loss have lost their sparkle for a while. I understand why they, too, seemed to be distant and isolated. It's like some secret society—a bit like having a baby. Not everyone has a baby, and therefore not everyone will understand that rush of feelings you get when your baby is born; that burst of love for this tiny being. Likewise, until you are orphaned, and at whatever age you are when that happens—until that has happened, it is difficult to articulate the cavern that appears inside you. Only recognizing that, and trying to accept the loss, and that this deep hole within you will always be there; only that acceptance will eventually allow you to move on.

You never forget, because they're not far from your mind, but you look around at others you know who have been in the same situation, and you think to yourself that they got through it, so it must be okay in the end. There must be a level you reach from which you can move forwards.

People say that those with dogs in their life seem to recover more quickly. Dogs give us a reason to get up in the morning; they give us a reason to open that front door, and go out of the house to be with other people; they give us a reason to face the world.

Many people are delayed in realizing the benefit of having a dog in their life. For an array of circumstances, some never do, simply because the time never feels right to take the plunge and have your first dog. Some do, though, and often later on in life—and one thing that is common to most of them, is that their life changes forever.

Sheena is one of my great friends. She's not really a very doggie person, or I should say she never used to be. Until recently that is.

She is in her mid-fifties and has a long-term history of allergies, one to dog hairs included in that list. One morning she popped over from her nearby house, and stayed perhaps a little longer than she had intended (for planned visits she used to always load up on antihistamines).

Lucy decided that, visitor having an allergy or not having an allergy, Sheena was her new best friend, and she was going to deposit herself on the sofa right next to her; not only sit next to her, but sit there enthusiastically licking her wrist. I offered to move Lucy away, but Sheena was fascinated by the fact that Lucy was licking an area on the side of her wrist where she had an extensive patch of very sore dermatitis. This patch of dermatitis had been raw and flaking for a long time, despite her use of copious amounts of various creams.

Lucy continued to voraciously lick Sheena's wrist for several minutes until the area was bright red, at which point I insisted on moving the reluctant terrier from the sofa.

I didn't see Sheena for a few weeks after that, but when I did she was full of a tale of how, within days of Lucy's insistent and persistent licking, the area on her wrist began to heal. She said that really quickly after Lucy's 'treatment' the initially raw, flaky skin had healed, and a healthy skin she had not seen for some years was peeking through the pale pink hint of an old lesion.

I'd never advise anyone to allow a dog to lick any type of wound—the risks of infection are vast, but this wasn't the first time Lucy had done something like this. When she was still with Mum, one of my Sunday visits had seen Lucy repeatedly sniffing at an old motorbike wound on my shin. The accident had happened many years earlier and had required eleven stitches. In the weeks before this visit to Mum's it had become lumpy, but was a completely closed lesion. Her insistent sniffing encouraged me to see the doctor, and following a biopsy it appeared the lump was a piece of dead, fatty tissue. It was nothing to be concerned about and I was lucky, but the fact remains that Lucy had noticed it.

Many other dogs also seem to have the ability to sense when something is medically out of synch with their human companions—or visitors in Sheena's case. In both these situations, Lucy was apparently drawn to that difference in the tissue's structure. She knew there was something not quite right. It is thought that many dogs have this ability, but that they don't think we're particularly interested in the information they have to offer. And so, in most situations, they just don't bother letting us know.

Peggy and Ralph don't do this so much—except for a bizarre habit they have of getting restless and sometimes whining whenever either Bob or I need a nocturnal visit to the toilet. Ralph's indicator at this point is to shake his head and you are woken by the flapping of his ears; Peggy's is to whine—these are the same indicators they use when they themselves want to go to the toilet. When we offer either dog the chance to go out to the garden, they simply lie back down again—so we figure it must be us they're telling. It could all be a coincidence, but both Bob and I have noticed a distinct pattern. Perhaps when we're getting to the stage where we need to go, we get restless, and that's what they're picking up on. Who knows? It's certainly an odd thing.

Lucy does this nocturnal indicating too, only with her already being on the bed, she will come and nudge you or tap at you with her paw to wake you. She really does seem to have some kind of canine aptitude for it. I sometimes think that with my kidney transplant and the side-effects of the medications I take, I must be a human of great medical contradictions to Lucy, but I feel some comfort in knowing we have our own little diagnostic dog in the house.

Lucy's not the first dog we've loved who has done this: Jack my big, black lurcher, who comforted me through the nights when I was on peritoneal dialysis—he always seemed to know when I needed his help. He woke me one night when a blood vessel had ruptured in my abdomen and I needed to go to the hospital. It wasn't a dire emergency, but it could so easily have been.

Dillon, the dog who was Anthony's companion from the age of eleven, and who saw him through to his twenties, was nicknamed 'Dr. Dill' for his tendency to seek out and want to lick wounds, bruises, or any old sore patch—on us or on the other dogs. While we humans appreciated (but politely declined) his efforts, the other dogs had varying responses, from a low growl to, in some cases, greater exposure of the offending wound or sore area so he could properly 'clean' it for them!

Indeed, it has been known for some time of the medical benefits of dogs. In their human companions they help to reduce blood pressure, heart rate, the likelihood of depression, and as already mentioned, they increase the circulating levels of the nurturing hormone oxytocin.

As time goes by, more benefits to our relationship with the dog are being realized, including their being able to detect fine alterations in our body's chemistry. In the last few decades they have shown they can detect the early onset of medical emergencies such as impending diabetic comas; indicating to the person before they even know themselves that their blood sugar level is low.

They can also predict epileptic convulsions so the person they live with knows to make themselves safe. In Addison's disease it seems they can predict an impending convulsion caused by a person's adrenal glands not producing enough cortisol.

The world is full of so many examples of this great mutual connection we have with dogs: dogs that have rescued people from fire, from water, from mountains, from earthquake devastation.

I am in constant awe of this species with whom we have chosen to share our lives; every day I feel humbled by their presence and hope for all dogs (and other animals) that there will come a time when their existence will be internationally appreciated.

Returning to the story of Sheena—shortly after her impromptu healing session with Lucy, she had found herself a dog. Her new little dog, and the latest addition to the contingent of dogs living locally, is Buster. He is a curly-coated, chocolate and white puppy.

So Sheena has set out on her journey with her first canine companion. I am sure he will be a great new friend for Ralph and Peggy. For obvious reasons I don't mention Lucy in this context, as we are yet to see what she will think of this new dog who is living in our midst. We're sure she'll let us know just as soon as she has decided. For the time being we have to wait, though, because Buster is still on house and garden arrest while he waits for his vaccines to provide him with the necessary immune response which will allow him to go and mix with the local canine community.

That human-animal bond that so many of us have

known for so very long exists between our species and other animals is, indeed, especially strong between human and dog. I am so happy that my friend has succumbed to the joy of canine companionship. I am sure she'll never regret it.

Friday April 22nd

Dog Beds and Imposters

Lucy

They have large beds, the other two.

Don't get me wrong, my bed is mighty fine for little old me, but theirs? Well, I can lie on my side and strrrreeeetch myself out until I extend to twice my body's length, and still the tips of my carefully-manicured nails don't touch the edges.

I felt the people needed to know that it really wasn't on that those two, just because they're big dogs, should have big beds when, just because I'm small, I get a much smaller one. I mean, I know I sleep on the human bed at night time, but again, that's really not the point.

I decided I would have to do something about this because it was really bugging me. So, every time they popped into the bedroom to fetch something they'd forgotten, or to fix their hair or brush their teeth, I followed them. I then made a point of sidling over to Peggy's bed, lying on my side, and demonstrating to them just how good it would be if I had one of those massive beds all to myself.

They clearly noticed, because they went out and purchased a large soft bed for me, just like Peggy's one—the same size and everything. I've not slept in it just yet though. Noooo, not at all. Why would I do that? It's just the principle of the whole thing—they simply needed to know how unfair they were being.

There's a new dog in the street. He belongs to that person who had the sore part that I fixed. He's been there a while now; I could smell his presence for ages and wondered why he was hiding himself away. We eventually met him recently when we were out for a walk. He's just young, and I can see that, but I wish he would behave! He spends all his time standing up on his back paws and waving his front feet at me. The first time I saw him do it, my eyes nearly popped out of my head. I growled at him, just to let him know that dogs shouldn't do what he was doing, but he ignored my growl. So I pulled my lips right up above my teeth and warned him with my eyes, but still he ignored me.

I can see I am going to have to think carefully about how I deal with that one—he's a monster! At least the other dogs around these parts back off when I tell them to.

As for Ralph, the weather is heating up again and he's doing that thing where he wants to hog all the sunny, warm places in the house. I want to record right here, right now, that this is not going to happen. Those sunny spots are mine!

Sunday May 1st

A New Dawn—Two Years On and Counting

Clare

I didn't notice Mum's ageing. I think that subconsciously I knew, but I ignored her slowing down, and all that the obvious degeneration of her body signified. As humans do we do that? Does it take a stark downward decline in someone's health and appearance for us to properly notice our loved ones are getting closer to the day on which they will leave us? Is it some sort of innate, protective mechanism we've evolved to have, just so we don't waste precious energy on grieving until the time is right for us to do so?

It's strange the things which, after someone dies, you remember and miss about them. In her later years, Mum would leave a trail of evidence in her wake of her having been around. She used to drop paper tissues on the floor. They would fall out of her cardigan pockets or from up her sleeve.

When Martin and I were children, we were never allowed out of the house without a tissue secured in the cuff of our shirt, blouse, cardigan or jumper. I guess that some habits remain with a person for the whole of their life. One key thing that did alter with this habit, though, and one which the dogs loved as Mum got older, was the fact that her scattered pieces of tissue often contained small chunks of food!

She used to go to church every weekend, and was worried about having a sugar-low while she was there. To overcome this, she carefully wrapped up crackers or biscuits. Invariably, she would forget they were in her pockets, up her sleeve, or tucked in her bag, and this did not go unnoticed by the dogs—especially Peggy.

With Peggy having the long, pointed face she has been blessed with, she frequently didn't even wait for tissues to fall to the floor. Her philosophy whenever Mum was around was that, if you have a long, pointed muzzle that fits neatly inside the old woman's pocket or up the woman's sleeve, then why would you not at least try? Needless to say, her enthusiastic searches often resulted in successful gatherings of human food.

Tissues also used to find themselves accidentally falling down the sides of the sofa cushions, and after Mum's visits it was always a race between us and Peggy to recover the pieces of tissue and their contents. How I miss those pieces of tissue. I am sure (for very different reasons) that so, too, does Peggy.

Mum had never recovered from losing my dad back in 1971. Yes, she had remarried, but that marriage never lived up to her expectations, because all there had ever really been for her was Dad. In the end, she spent more than four decades of her life mourning him. Before she died, and in a moment when she and I were sharing memories of the times when my brother and I were little, and Dad had still been with us, I said that one day she would see him again.

One day.

In an effort to ease the pain that's what so many of us say to one another isn't? One day we'll all meet again in some distant place not of this world.

The answer she gave still chills me. She said that if they did ever 'meet' again, how would they know? Would they remember the people they had been? The way they had been when they were together? She was convinced that they would never actually know that they had been Mo and Tony. I guess that was on her mind in the months following our conversation. I am sure in the time she spent alone, that when she thought of him, she wondered.

This is just as I now wonder about whether they are now together—and if so, *do* they know? Do they remember who they once were? Are they in some paradise in the skies surrounded by our other loved ones who have passed on? Are they having a cup of tea and watching over us all? Is there a great big garage in the sky, and Dad is lying underneath some oily car in some dirty overalls, while Mum waits for him to take her driving along some wild flower-flanked country lanes? Are they singing songs they're listening to on the radio, and laughing at memories of the life they had together here on Earth? Are they in some magical place accompanied by all the people, dogs, and cats they loved in their lifetime?

I look for signs in everything. I think that if they could, then perhaps they would try to get a message through to me? As I write this, the theme tune from the film *Ghost*, *Unchained Melody*, has just come on the radio. Perhaps it is a sign? You would not believe how often the song *Que sera sera*, Mum's funeral song, comes on the radio and I see it as a sign. But then, there are only so many times you can hear a song and think that perhaps this time it really is a symbol of their trying to communicate with you; only so many times you can feel something is a sign they are watching over us, before you eventually put it all down to pure coincidence.

These are worries and notions that I'm not sure dogs have. To them the radio is probably just a series of annoying bumps and bangs, and the connections we make to our lost loved ones are perhaps thoughts that are alien to our four-legged companions. But how can we possibly know what they think, or what they remember? If my voice really does trigger memories in Lucy, then perhaps music on the radio or signature tunes on the television do, too?

In two days it will be two years since she passed. This is now time to move on, time to focus on our quality of life and live in the present. Who knows what becomes of us all? That's the question about which generations of people have pondered. Every religion, every sector of society has its own belief, and really all any of us can do is wait it out. No amount of sorrow will bring them back. All we can do is just spend our life doing the things we love doing, while remembering the good times we had with those who have left us, and hope that one day we really will be together again.

Sunday July 3rd

Holiday time

Clare

The issue of Mum's ashes has reared its head again. We are off to Wales, and I have considered scattering them in the sea at Llandudno. That's where she honeymooned with my dad, so it seems to be the perfect choice. The only problem is that we are going to South Wales, and not to the north where Llandudno sits shaped by its limestone Great Orme and Little Orme, the two headlands that flank the bay.

Since having my bright idea, however, I've recently heard they're grazing sheep on the Great Orme. I feel that now I can't possibly go and scatter ashes up there, what with the potential for everything going wrong with the combination of ashes, dogs, sheep, and emotional humans, particularly when you also have the direction of the wind to worry about. Whatever I do, remembering that it is me who's been left with the responsibility for deciding, it has to be something that will go smoothly.

I also thought about scattering her ashes off the pier at Weston-Super-Mare. It isn't too much of a jaunt from South Wales to there, and we could just hop across the Severn Bridge into England. We had holidayed there as kids, so surely that was ideal? Or how about thinking right outside of the box and scattering her in Jersey? She loved Jersey. I do, too, and would like to go back there someday. She'd only been there once, when she was young and carefree and working for Cadbury. She and a bunch of girls had gone there as group from work and had the best time together—she used to talk of it so often. But the link to Jersey seemed somehow inadequate—it was such a long time ago and it would be difficult for all of us to go—especially the dogs.

Whether we end up taking Mum's ashes with us or not, we're going to Wales in our new camper—Victor. It's actually a Ford Transit van we're converting. Currently it's what you might call a 'work in progress' in that, while it now has windows in the back, and nothing dividing the cab from the rear, that's as far as we've got with the conversion. Luckily we have booked a cottage, so all's well for the holiday—we won't have to snuggle down with the dogs in a cold van. And if previous trips to Wales are anything to go by, just like a home from home, I expect it will rain.

Saturday July 23rd

Wonderful Wales

Clare

We headed off to South Wales with the dogs in tow. Having the van to go down in, while also having the cottage booked, did in the end make us feel as though we were sort of cheating.

When Anthony found he was going to be at a loose end for a couple of weeks, he decided he would tag along and we'd all have some quality time together. A few days before we left, though, he decided that instead he was going to stay at home and work on a music project he wanted to complete during his summer break. To keep him company, we decided to leave one of the dogs at home with him.

So, which dog to leave at home with him? Therein lay our dilemma.

Peggy is the dog who is the most bonded to Anthony, but Ralph definitely depends on having Peggy around, so we knew that separating them would be difficult. As we got them only six weeks apart, I guess that since then they've been through everything together. We also know for sure that Ralph depends on me, and would be awfully restless if I left him at home for a week. I know that is terribly anthropomorphic, but a little anthropomorphism can go a long way in our human-animal bond.

With our dog politics straight in our heads, we reluctantly decided to leave Lucy at home. She would receive lots of love and all her creature comforts while we were away, and we'd make it up to her once we got home. Leaving was difficult, and I almost relented and bundled her into the car, but then I remembered how she and Anthony would have lots of nice walks and quality time together, and left her with him. After all, it was only going to be for a week.

And so, while we went off exploring castles, beaches and forests, they stayed behind and manned the fort—our own little castle (well, modern house) in Scotland. Once we'd left she was restless for a day or so. I imagine she had the right to be a little fed up—her two best buddies (even though she doesn't treat them as such) had vanished off the face of the earth.

Setting off on our holiday in our partially-completed camper van, we felt we'd achieved something we had wanted to do, and had talked about doing, for so long. There we were, the two of us perched in the front, the dogs relaxing on their comfy beds in the back; all quite happy. A feeling of calm came over me—perhaps a little prematurely.

Whenever we're on our travels we have to be extremely careful with Ralph and how we go about doing things.

Although more than five years have passed since we got him, he's still nervous. Stopping at a service station on a long journey, for instance, is not as simple as it might be with a dog who hasn't been through whatever he experienced before. We really don't know what he went through; we can only surmise that he had a pretty tough time.

The first service station we stopped at on our (what ended up being) eight and a half hour expedition from southern Scotland to South Wales, was extremely noisy. The thunder of the trucks going past, along with the busy station itself which had masses of people and cars all competing for space, were not at all conducive to Ralph's liking of a peaceful life.

I considered at one point that in actual fact HE would have been the ideal companion to have left back at home with Anthony for the week. The calmness would have suited him. Lucy wouldn't have been the least bit perturbed by a silly service station—it would have been an opportunity for her to have intimidated any other dogs that were passing through! But we'd made our decision, and here we were with Ralph and Peggy, along with the aforementioned heavy trucks roaring past on the motorway. Peggy was dutifully having a pee beside a solitary tree we'd found amid the mayhem. But Ralph, well, once we had eased him out of the van, he froze to the spot and had no intention of going to the toilet, moving, or doing anything we needed him to.

It took a while to coax him back into the van, and I vowed to never again take him to a service station that was on the main stretch of a busy motorway. I think that as time has gone by, and because he has in many ways become more confident, my sense of complacency has led me to believe that he can cope. I naively expected that in that situation he would just hop out of the van, think to himself, 'Okay, cool, what a great day this is—time for a pee-break, and perhaps a dog biscuit or two?' Ralph has this way, though, of luring you into a false sense of security.

So no, absolutely not, he was definitely not going to do either of these things. There was no way he was going to go to the toilet or be pacified with a dog biscuit. Thankfully, about an hour later we found some services off an A-road, rather than a motorway, and he managed both going to the toilet and a biscuit!

It rained for much of the first few days of our time in Wales. At the cottage the rain bounced off the roof of the conservatory, and we wondered whether it would ever stop. We tried to time our excursions so they coincided with the short periods of sunshine, and sometimes managed to succeed; at other times we arrived back soaking wet, along with two soggy, very fed up dogs. We've never been such avid watchers of the weather forecasts! There were many occasions when we thanked our lucky stars we were sleeping in a nice cozy bed in a cottage, rather than our partially-completed camper van. We were also extremely grateful that Bob had packed our wellies.

Wales is so very beautiful, not unlike Scotland—and the place we stayed was no exception.

There were a lot of horses around by the cottage, and Ralph and Peggy completely ignored them—even the ones that followed us as we ambled alongside their fields. Like dogs do, horses forge powerful bonds with one another, and we unfortunately discovered that two of the horses' days together were numbered because they were being sold on to homes where they would be living as single pets. This made me sad, as these two beautiful, majestic animals were clearly so very fond of one another. This was clear by the way in which they played and frolicked around their fields. Horses are herding animals and benefit so greatly from the company of others.

I so often feel incredibly saddened by the way we humans have such power over animals. It's as though people believe our apparent 'dominion' over them has somehow given us the right to break up animal friendships, using them for our own entertainment and profit.

These thoughts of animals being separated reminded me of how we had left Lucy back home with Anthony, but at least I knew she would be all right. I was sure she was being absolutely spoilt! I phoned home every day, sometimes twice a day, to see how they were doing.

The responses I got from Anthony were similar in each conversation:

'Yes, she's fine.'

'Yes, she's been for a walk—and been fed.'

'Yes, she's eating her food.'

'Yes, she's had some treats as well.'

'Yes, I think she really is missing you.'

'Yes, I'm sure she'll forgive you!'

'No, I don't think you should talk to her because you'll just upset her!'

The voice on the other end of the phone sounded weary—weary from his music-writing and playing, I was sure. I'm positive it wasn't my repeated questioning that was bothering him. He loves animals—loves them with as great a passion as I do. He seems to get how they feel and how their emotions play out—his care of Lucy would be second to none.

Wales is a country that is very familiar to me. Whether you're in the north or the south, they both have so much to offer. I grew up in Birmingham and pretty much all my childhood holidays were spent in Wales, Weston-super-Mare or Cornwall, mostly Wales though. The long, sandy beaches with their abundant sand dunes allow you to escape from the world and take cover in pockets of sand created by time.

As we drove around the Welsh hills and valleys, and alongside cliff tops that overhang the golden-sanded bays, I sensed nostalgic echoes of years gone by. I felt I'd been there before. Not, I don't think anyway, in a reincarnation kind of way, but more in a way that I was there, actually there, in this lifetime. I'd been there as me, but a much younger me. I was there multiple times on those familiar roads, and dipping my toes in those familiar blue-green waves. Our time in Wales allowed me to absorb those feelings of remembrance. Those had been different times with different people and different dogs, but still, the beauty and ambience I remembered from Wales was deep inside me.

We always holidayed with our dogs when I was growing up. We would take whichever dogs we happened to have at the time and go off exploring secluded bays. We played in the sea with those dogs and had the best fun, creating memories for our futures. In my, what could be rose-tinted reminiscences, the weather was always scorching hot, and we would race into the sea to cool off. Our canine friends would lie with their long, pink tongues lolling outside of their mouths, attracting scratchy, gritty sand. From a warm, plastic bottle we would replenish the fresh water in their bowl, which they would lap at enthusiastically; spilling precious drops and creating water stains in the golden sands.

As we passed along these hedge-kissed roads, and

gazed at the skies which were sometimes obscured by mountains and cliffs, I recalled once more how my friend said that you remember people in different places; that you don't necessarily need a particular place to go and visit. A smell, a flower, a particular type or time of day, all of these can make you think of them. Watching the Welsh scenery flashing past, I remembered. I recalled times when I was there with Mum; times when she and I breathed the same air, loved the same dogs, and loved doing the same things.

A food can make you think of lost loved ones too—for me it's peanut butter and banana sandwiches, jam and banana sandwiches, salt and vinegar crisps, or baked potatoes (but not all of them together). Simple foods such as those, often the sight and smell of them evoke memories from times long ago.

For me, those memories are entangled with memories of the dogs we loved when those were the foods we regularly ate. The banana and peanut butter or jam sandwiches were when we were children, and so I associate them with Prince the epileptic dog, and Beauty the dog who came along after him. The baked potatoes came later, along with Mum's passion for salt and vinegar crisps, and both of those passions led her through the eras of Kerry, Skye, Gail, and then of course, Lucy.

Lamb chops were also associated with Prince. This was because of the time when I was twelve years old, and he was sitting beside me with his head on my lap while I was eating my dinner. I looked down at his beautiful brown eyes and back to my plate with the meat on it, and something clicked in my mind. That was *my* moment—the penny-dropping moment when I wondered what the difference was between farm animals and dogs. To my mind, from that point, there was none. That day I became vegetarian. Twenty-five years on I became vegan. That was far too many years later, and I shall always regret that I didn't make the big connection all in one go, and become vegan back in 1977 when I was just twelve years old.

My age twelve decision to become vegetarian was something the rest of my family struggled with. This was especially so for Mum who, being in charge of the shopping, would often find herself having to scrutinize food packets on my behalf. In the end, she gave me a small weekly budget to take to the health food shop to buy the foods I needed. I think she thought it was a phase I was going through. Attitudes were different then, and veggie food availability was just not as easy as it is today.

Holidays always evoke memories of other holidays, and on one of those holidays in Wales, Mum had tracked down a tin of vegetable soup for me. As soon as I tasted it, I knew it had some kind of meat in it. I asked to see the can, but the can had miraculously disappeared—my stepfather had apparently already taken it to the communal caravan site bins. Insisting there was nothing wrong with the soup, Mum tried to get me to eat it. There was no way on this Earth I was going to, though, and I pushed the soup away from me, choosing to eat some toast and peanut butter, along with my special veggie margarine. Once cool enough, the soup was given to Prince, who gratefully lapped it up without a second thought.

That night I had a vivid dream that there were chickens suspended from the roof of the caravan above my put-you-up bed, and told Mum about it the following morning. The holiday passed with no more offers of questionable vegetarian soup. It was only many years later that Mum admitted the soup had indeed had meat in it—and it *had* been chicken. It is strange the things you remember when you have time to stop and think—I hadn't thought about the soup saga for years. Our holiday in Wales definitely reminded me of Mum's great soup betrayal!

In the end we didn't take Mum's ashes to Wales, but left them back in Scotland still nestled deep inside the giant lavender pot. We are now more than two years beyond that point when everything in our lives changed. We are two years and a couple of months beyond the point when Lucy came to live with us, and still we can't decide what to do with those ashes! They are the remnants of a life that once was; the remnants of all she had been. Except, that is, for the parts of her which live on in the memories of those who loved her; those who saw the beauty in her laughter, her generosity of spirit, and the intense way she felt about the world—a world which, for her, had been tainted by what she had experienced. I guess that's one of the reasons why I am finding it so difficult to let go. Whether her ashes will stay there indefinitely, I don't know, but at least she is close by.

I have some of her habits, I know I do. A prime example is the way in which the dogs take advantage of me, and will always look towards me as being the most likely person to give in to them. If they stare at me for just ten more seconds when they are after something, then it is likely I'll dutifully walk to the treats cupboard to find them something tasty to eat. Lucy used to do that with Mum, too.

Mum also had a habit of perching her over-stuffed large bag on her lap and ferreting through it for something that had likely been in there (probably festering) for at least six months. I do that as well, however hard I try not to in an attempt to fight my genes!

So, there we were in Wales with all those memories, but without Anthony, without Lucy, without Mum's ashes. We missed Anthony and Lucy and thought that perhaps Lucy should have come with us. She's a real testament to her erratic genetics. She is confident to the point that, if she were human, you would describe her as being assertive.

There are things on holiday that Ralph struggled to do

(or absolutely wouldn't do in a couple of cases); things which Lucy would have done without a second thought. Lucy is good company, she is constantly attentive. Ralph demands your attention in a different way: where Lucy protects us; we protect Ralph. But we unconditionally love all three dogs. They are different in their personalities and their needs, and that is the beauty of rescue dogs.

When you're holidaying with dogs you have to carefully plan each excursion. The Internet becomes your friend as you wade through tourist web pages adding '+ dogs welcome' to all your searches. This is lest you get there having assumed 'surely they allow dogs into that beach/garden/forest/ruined castle!' If you don't plan well, you could have a seventy or eighty mile round trip from your lodgings, often along narrow country roads, resulting in your heart sinking as you take in the words on that notice which is feared by all dog owners holidaying with their dogs: '*No Dogs Allowed.*' Or else you find someone looking you and your dog up and down from the safety of their kiosk, and telling you that under no circumstances are dogs allowed inside. In the past this has happened to us on a few occasions, and so now we scrutinize tourist information before we go.

So we found all our dog-friendly beaches, gardens, forests, and ruined castles. And then, living in the 21st century as we now do, instead of circling interesting points on an OS map, we avidly put our intended post codes into our trusted satellite navigation system. The local attractions were ours for the taking, and off we went to explore them.

Unfortunately, as usual, our dear Ralph had other ideas!

Nestled in the beautiful hills and valleys of Llanelli, is Kidwelly Castle. It is a mediaeval castle a little famous for its appearance in Monty Python's Holy Grail. The castle's appearance in the film is very brief, however, which is something we discovered when we returned home and re-watched the film. Apparently the main castle in the film is Doune Castle in our homeland of Scotland. But, there we were, oblivious to this fact and heading towards the castle, excited at its link to Monty Python, and equally curious at the prospect of exploring its depths.

Ralph was not that enamoured with the castle, first of all with the entrance to this (I must say truly dog-friendly) castle. His first problem was that there was slippery flooring in the entrance to the shop, which is also the entrance to the castle, and Ralph absolutely does not cope on slippery floors. The lady working in the shop, however, kindly came around and let us in through the side gate.

So, we had not had a wasted trip, we were in, and with it not yet being English or Welsh school holidays, it was fairly quiet. We cheerfully ambled along the grass-flanked path and everyone, including Ralph, was happy.

Not for long though!

We stopped outside the grey stone walls and reminisced about Monty Python. I was trying to get some good shots of the entrance, so we lingered outside to wait for the people in front of us to clear from the entrance because they were spoiling my picture! Unfortunately, while I was so keenly trying to frame my shot, it seems that Ralph had spotted something neither Bob nor I had seen—at the actual entrance to the castle itself was a wooden bridge which crossed what would have been the moat.

When he gets frightened by something, Ralph usually goes right up to it before he gets worried, or before he tries to make a hasty retreat. Often we've spotted whatever it is before he has and can take evasive action. In this case, though, whether he'd seen another dog nervously walking across the bridge while we were so distracted with taking the picture, and had thought to himself: 'Not on your Nellie,' I don't know, but we got about ten feet away from the wooden planks, and he froze to the spot. He then dug in his heels, and looked up at us as if to say, 'I am absolutely NOT going across that bridge, however many dog chews, biscuits, or walks you promise me!'

And he wouldn't.

So we walked around the external walls of the castle in an attempt to find another way in, but there wasn't one. I guess that was the beauty of a moat for our Welsh ancestors, but for us, on that day, the moat and its bridge were going to be a psychological stumbling block for Ralph. So we tried to encourage him to go over it again, but there was no way he was going within ten feet of even the start of the bridge.

And so, Ralph's will being much greater than ours, and the fact that he is a big, strong dog (Bob did consider carrying him over the bridge, and he could have managed it, but we decided it would be too stressful for Ralph), we decided to take it in turns to go in.

First of all, Peggy and I went in for a look around—which Peggy, quite surprisingly, was really into. For some reason she particularly liked the mediaeval oven and, bizarrely, she went over to investigate it a few times before we came back out to relieve Bob of Ralph-watching duties. While I pottered about with the two dogs on the grass by the bridge, Bob went in on his own so he could climb the staircase and wave to us from the highest windows.

What was so frustrating about this tale of Ralph and his woes, was what happened once we were all together again. We decided to go for a riverside walk just beside the castle. Fewer than two minutes into the walk, there in front of us was a rickety wooden bridge. This was not unlike the one over the moat, only this one was even less stable. As soon as I saw it, I said to Bob, 'Oh well, we'd better go the other way.' But then, without a second's hesitation, Ralph quite happily walked across it. This was not in a nervous way, but he happily trotted across it as confidently as Peggy did! Ralph can be so very frustratingly unpredictable.

Wales is lovely . . . and after the bridge experience, both dogs appeared to relish our trips out in the van to go and sightsee. This was helped by us deciding to give any more castles a miss, mainly due to Ralph's varied appreciation of footbridges. In South Wales there are many long, sandy beaches, and there's so much fascinating history. The area has been shaped by time and also through its coal and iron industries. The hedgerow along much of the roadside in Wales provides a necessary haven for garden birds, along with privacy and seclusion for the fields, gardens, and woodland beyond.

Dylan Thomas' poetry was penned in the gorgeous bay of Laugharne. There's a magnificent view of the green-tinged ocean that must have every day been his for the taking, while he sat writing in the shed above the boathouse. The dogs appreciated the walk along the paths towards the boathouse and beyond it into the woods. I'm not sure dogs appreciate quite so much the wonder of a famous Welsh poet's inspirational bay.

The time was drawing closer to when we would return home. Missing Anthony and missing Lucy, we decided to leave for Scotland a few days early. We had pretty much seen what we went down there for, and had missed them both very much.

One of our key reasons for choosing South Wales as our holiday destination was that we wanted to visit the Six Bells miners' monument in Abertillery, so this is where we stopped on our way home. This twenty-meter statue is in memory of the forty-five men, some of them related to one another: fathers, sons, cousins, uncles, and grandfathers, who died after the gas explosion in the mine in 1960. As you stand next to the statue, feeling dwarfed and somehow insignificant, it reminds you of the shortness of life, and of how much we should value each day. The statue stands watching over the people of Abertillery, protecting by its presence those who still live there.

The dogs were grateful for the walk leading to the statue and, had it been cooler, we could have walked for miles, but Peggy's not very tolerant of the heat, and so we returned to the camper for our long journey home.

Sunday July 31st

Holidays—for Some Anyway

Lucy

Well, what DO you think about that? They disappeared for a while in that vehicle, the woman and the man. Not only that, they took Ralph and Peggy with them. I presume they took them with them anyway, because they did all disappear at the same time. I wasn't left alone though . . . Nooooo, not at all! Nooooo, I had the tall human to look after.

So, him and me, we kind of hung out together, and every now and then I brought him in line if he wasn't giving me biscuits at the right time, or if he'd missed the fact that it was time for us to go out for my check around the streets where we live. There was always a chance I would see that black and white Chester dog, or Buster the annoying pup who keeps on trying to jump at my face. Chester used to do that when he first arrived on the scene, but I soon told him. Even now I have to remind him from time to time with a sharp growl in the back of my throat.

While they were away I insisted on sleeping on the tall one's bed at night, which he didn't seem to mind. Other times we spent quite a lot of time together while he was making a lot of noise and was wearing strange ears on the side of his head. When he wore those, his head was nodding all the time, which I thought was a bit weird! A lot weird, in fact.

He has this machine that is really loud which he hits with sticks while he is bobbing his head. It's all very worrying, and quite violent really. Then there's the strange object with all the strings on it, which, when he finally manages to detach himself from it, seems to spend a lot of time taking up space where I want to lie down.

While they were away he was quite obliging, though, and gave me plenty of fuss and walks. There were quite a lot of treats and games of 'fetch' as well. It was nice not to have to compete for food with Peggy long-face, but in some ways I missed her and Ralph.

It was really quite miserable of them to go away without us. They're back now, and I'm making the most of their guilt by getting as many treats and cuddles as possible.

Saturday August 20th

Forgiven and Life Goes On

Clare

There were so many times when we were away that I missed them both. I missed Anthony and I missed Lucy, but I found consolation in telling myself he was busy doing his music, and Lucy was busy keeping him in check. When we returned home early it was to see them and, I guess subconsciously, redeem ourselves a little. We came home the quick way and were keen to spend time with Anthony for the remaining few days he would be at home. I found myself desperate for us all to spend quality time together, because really that's the most important thing isn't it? Time?

Bob and I had thoroughly enjoyed Wales, but feeling there was a part of us missing was difficult. I think it would have been different had we always intended for the holiday to have just been the two of us, but we hadn't, and all the plans we'd had just changed.

Having lived away from home for some years now, Anthony wasn't bothered by our absence. And, of course, Lucy forgave us—dogs do. That's one of the things that makes them so special to us humans—they accept us with all our imperfections. They accept us as we are and don't mind what we wear, whether we have make-up on, whether we've got a lot of money, or whether we live in a nice house. They just want to love us, and all they ask is for us to love them back. Just love, some exercise, food and water, veterinary care, and company. That is all. In return, the love they give us is intoxicatingly abundant. They altruistically enhance our lives in so many ways that it is difficult for any human to deliver due reciprocation.

We came back from our holiday and walked the dogs together, played board games, and watched a TV box set and a few films. There was the simple joy of us all being together again.

Having Lucy by our sides, loving us, and paying us the undivided attention she does, it made me realize even more how much I love that little dog. I've never really been a 'little dog' person, always having dogs no smaller than a crossed collie, and I don't think I would ever choose a small dog over a larger one, but I've gradually seen the appeal.

Lucy has the most interesting character. Despite her apparent bossiness, she is incredibly affectionate. She also has a confidence not seen in many larger dogs, and she has the attitude necessary to get her through. I wonder if this is what has helped her in her apparent recovery from losing Mum. I wonder whether her strength of character has been helping her all along. I wonder whether it is this that helped her to pick herself up and get on with beginning her life in a new home. Our home.

I hope that on some level my writing this down will help someone who has lost their own loved one; or it may help someone who is carefully trying to integrate a loved one's companion animal into their own family. I know that everyone experiences grief at some point—it's the natural order of things, but it can be hard to know that the feelings you have are normal; that the pain and the nightmares will ease; that things will get better. You'll never forget who that person was; they'll always be a part of you, and recognizing that is perhaps part of the way towards healing yourself.

As I write these last few pages, as is his wont, gentle Ralph is lying in the natural warmth of the rays of sunshine beaming through the French windows. Beautiful, serene Peggy is lying on her back with her legs stretched vertically, filling the sofa so there's no space for any other being, be they human or dog. Lucy, sweet little Lou, is in the sunshine on another sofa, attempting the same greyhound-style of 'lying on your back with your legs in the air' position, which somehow doesn't look quite so elegant when it's demonstrated by a short-legged terrier-type. There is plenty of sunshine to go around, and today Ralph and Lucy don't need to nudge one another out of the way.

The French windows are open, and there's a strong breeze drifting in from the garden. The weather forecast says it is going to be windy for a few days, and one of the fruit trees lost a branch last night. The chimes in the garden are chiming more than usual, and the lavender in Mum's pot is waving in the wind. I should really close the door, because despite the sunshine there is now a chill in the air. I don't want to, though, as having the doors open makes me feel close to her. I am now so glad we didn't scatter her miles away from here. Wales is a long way away and it would have felt strange. I am glad she is here with us. I don't know whether we'll always keep her ashes here in the garden, but for now it feels right.

The sparrows and finches are out there on the bird feeders. The crows, jackdaws, pigeons, and a herring gull are feeding on the bird table or from the ground. A little earlier Peggy wandered out there to sniff around the garden and didn't chase them—perhaps she sees they have enough to contend with today, what with that blustering wind. The birds stayed while she was there, perhaps out of desperation. Every now and then they do fly up into the sky, bracing themselves against the wind, and flapping their wings twice as hard as usual.

I wonder whether Mum really is somewhere that she is able to watch over us; I wonder whether she can see this scene, how we are doing, and that her little Lucy is safe and well.

Lucy's definitely a handful, and I suspect she'll remain so until she is old and grey. Or I suppose it's possible she will never slow down, some terriers don't. We shall always have this little tyrant in our midst, until one day she, too, will leave us. In her time with us she'll have made that mark on our lives, just like all the other dogs we have taken into our hearts and loved. She's certainly also made her mark on the lives of Peggy and Ralph. Indeed, their lives will never be the same again. But I don't think they mind. Not anymore.

And when eventually this little dog does leave us, we'll miss the way she follows us around, and the way she watches all our moves. We'll miss the way she comforts us when we're poorly, and rejoices with us when we're happy. She's a little dog with that typical little-dog-big-attitude, and while she was never meant to be ours, we're so very glad she is. We're grateful that in her, for the time being anyway, we still have that little piece of Mum.

OTHER BOOKS BY CLARE COGBILL

A Dog Like Ralph
. . . A Book for Anyone Who has Ever Loved a Rescue Dog

The true story of Ralph—a rescue dog with a difficult past—who loves other dogs, is frightened of people and cars, and mesmerized by cats, rabbits and 'Santa Please Stop Here' signs. Clare, his new human companion, tells with equal amounts of humour and sadness about the challenges and joys of having him as a companion.

His story is partly told through his eyes and describes how what he may have experienced before has affected how he interacts with those in his new 'forever' home. When Ralph's compatriots, Peggy and Luella (Lucy to her friends), enter his life, it becomes clear that they have their own 'version of events' to add to the story!

Clare also writes about the pitfalls of a society that has resulted in Ralph being the way he is, and of how small changes could transform the plight of abandoned dogs. This book is a tribute to the rescue dog.

A Dog Like Ralph gives some of the back story to *The Diary of a Human and a Dog (or Three)*, but it is not necessary to read *A Dog Like Ralph* first.

A Soldier Like Jack

Like millions of other young men, Jack was plunged into a war which was to change his life, and the lives of his loved ones, forever. Jack's war would take him to Salonika (Thessaloniki), in Greece.

Jack's wife, Grace, tells the harrowing story of what happened to the men and the families they left behind. It traces their lives from the time of Jack and Grace's marriage in 1912, until Grace's death in 1957.

This is a true story based on the lives of the author's great grandparents, Jack and Grace Cogbill.

Lilac Haze

You don't remember your childhood in detail, so your memories thirty or forty years on have become hazy; times you had back then are painted in colours that have become distorted.

This is a love story. In the end, anyway, that's what it will be. A love story gives you hope: whatever you have lost; whatever you have to gain. For me, as someone on daily kidney dialysis, when an offer of a kidney came along which I couldn't possibly refuse, there was everything to gain.

But the past has a way of interfering with what seems to be the right path . . . and how do you ever in this life repay such an immeasurable debt?

ABOUT THE AUTHOR

Clare Cogbill was born in the mid-1960s, and like many youngsters from an early age she developed a deep passion for animals and their welfare. She had fifteen years experience of working with domesticated animals in rescue shelters, and as a qualified veterinary nurse in both welfare and private practice environments before, in 1991, becoming a lecturer in animal care and veterinary nursing. These days she mostly teaches companion animal welfare.

While animals have always been her greatest interest, she also loves to read, preferring biographies to fiction, and where those books contain some reference to the human-animal bond, all the better. She also enjoys reading books that have been made into films, but still can't quite work out whether it's better to read the book or to see the film first!

Clare lives in Scotland with her husband, three rescue dogs, and two rescued hamsters. She has one son who has now flown the nest and is following his own dreams.

If you've enjoyed any of my books, do please get in touch through Facebook or Goodreads.
Reviews on Amazon and/or Goodreads are very gratefully received.
Thank you so much for reading our story.

Made in the USA
Columbia, SC
23 July 2018